Are You Ready to Hike the Pacific Crest Trail?

JIM HILL

This book tells about my thru-hike of the Pacific Crest Trail to the best of my memory.

Contents

Dedication..iii

1 The Desert...1

2 The Sierras..39

3 Northern California..64

4 Oregon..92

5 Washington...112

About the Author...139

1 THE DESERT

When I finished hiking the Appalachian Trail in 2009, I thought it would fade into a pleasant memory. It had more of an impact on my life than I expected.

I spent a lot of time remembering the beautiful mountains, the sounds of gently flowing streams, the smell of pines, the coolness of their shade on a hot day, the friendships that developed, and the good times I had along the way. I realized hiking the Appalachian Trail had been so much fun I wanted to have another adventure. I decided to hike the Pacific Crest Trail.

The Pacific Crest Trail starts at the Mexican border in Campo, California. It winds 2,660 miles through the hot deserts and high mountains of California, around majestic, glacier covered volcanoes in Oregon, over meadows full of fragrant, colorful lupine and old growth forest in Washington, before ending at the Canadian border.

I started this hike with more questions and anxiety than I was willing to admit. When I hiked the Appalachian Trail I realized after the first week that this was something I really loved doing. I took to it like a duck to water. Prior to my hike I had read hiker's journals on TrailJournal.com. Many hikers talked about wanting to quit or actually did quit on their thru-hike attempt. After finishing my hike of the Appalachian Trail I couldn't fathom why anyone would want to quit. My attitude bordered on arrogance.

I attempted a thru-hike of the Pacific Crest Trail in 2011. Physically, I was in good condition. Mentally, I let things bother me that had never bothered me on the Appalachian Trail. I quit after four days.

When I started my 2012 hike of the Pacific Crest Trail I was wondering which hiker would show up. I also wasn't getting any younger. I was 62 when I hiked the Appalachian Trail. Now I was 65. Would my body hold up?

My trail name on the Appalachian Trail was Wingo. I decided to let the other hikers give me a trail name on the Pacific Crest Trail. To all the hikers I was Jim.

I started my hike on May 9th 2012. The bus dropped us off in the little town of Campo at 12:30 pm. A young, fresh faced, couple started with me. They looked super fit. They had tiny packs and were already trying to find ways to cut pack weight as they were talking on the bus. There was an eagerness and excitement on their faces.

We had to walk down a dirt road for about half an hour to get to the PCT monument. It was next to a high metal wall that divided Mexico and the US. At the monument I put my name and the date on the official PCT register and was on my way. I was so excited I forgot to have my picture taken. I waved to the young couple who were already on the Trail. I knew I would not see them again and had a feeling they would complete their thru-hike.

The rest of the day was hot, desert hiking. I had hardened my feet prior to the hike by walking each day, but the sandy, uneven, rocky pathway was already creating hot spots. I wanted to test my balance and decided to hike as long as I could without my hiking poles. That lasted about two miles. After coming close to falling a couple of times I realized how much I needed those poles. I had them shortened as far as they would go and tucked tightly in my backpack. Instead of opening the backpack and unloading it, I decided to pull the poles out. Neither of them would stay tightened for very long from then on. My legs complained on the uphill climbs. The sun was beating down and I was sweating profusely. Every couple of hours I would take a break and have some trail mix and Gatorade. Finally I made it to the top of the mountain and the pathway stayed on top for a while. There were long distance views in all directions.

As I was walking along admiring the view I just about stepped on a rattlesnake. It was a big one. It saw me before I saw it and began to rattle and coil. I couldn't stop my momentum and kept moving forward. This pissed it off and it rattled furiously! It was within a second of coiling enough to strike. My adrenaline was flowing like crazy and I shot out of its way. It continued to rattle at me for another fifty feet until I turned a corner and was out of sight. There were goose bumps on my arms.

I hiked at a steady pace and after a long downhill stretch, reached Hauser Canyon by 7:00 pm. I set up my tent next to a stream. It was pleasant listening to the gently flowing water. It was flowing almost too gently and so shallow it was hard to find a place to fill my water bottles. I wasn't sure if I should purify the water with my Aqua Mira drops or not. I opted to drink out of the stream. After dinner it was closing in on 8:30 pm and I decided to go to bed early and try for an early start the next morning.

Fifteen minutes later a loud helicopter slowly rumbled by. The PCT was a pathway for illegal immigrants and being only sixteen miles from the border and a water source, Hauser Canyon was an area the Border Patrol kept their eyes on. A half an hour later it slowly rumbled by in the opposite direction. It was a big helicopter. The ground shook as it went by.

A small dirt road was next to the stream but I knew I wasn't going to be bothered by traffic. There was a closed gate across the road. At 10:00 pm I heard a vehicle stop on the road twenty feet from my tent. I looked out. Two Border Patrol agents got out of their truck and chatted with each other for about ten minutes. Finally they left and I was able to get to sleep. I was awakened by movement and a flashlight shining on my tent.

"BORDER PATROL! YOU AND YOUR COMPANION COME OUT OF THE TENT!"

"I'm the only one in the tent."

"UNZIP THE TENT AND COME OUT!"

As I unzipped the tent he flashed his light into the tent to make sure I was the only one there.

"SHOW ME THE BOTTOM OF YOUR SHOES!"

Yes, sir. I'm a PCT thru-hiker. This is my first day on the Trail.

"Sorry to have bothered you. I've been following your footprints for the last five miles. I thought you were an illegal."

Once he established I wasn't an illegal he was courteous and even asked a few questions about my hike. By the time he left it was past midnight. I needed some sleep. I don't believe this! The helicopter came rumbling by again and I knew sooner or later it was going to make its sweep and come back. Which it did....

Finally around 2:00 am I was back asleep. I was only ten feet from the Trail and awakened by feet moving quickly and quietly past my tent. Illegals!

I know I said that I wanted to have an adventure but this was getting ridiculous.

I started the next morning a little bit groggy and I'm sure you can understand why. In the desert you need to start early in the cool of the morning. Once the sun comes up it gets hot fast. There was an immediate, long climb out of Hauser Canyon that seemed to go on forever. It took me three hours to hike the four miles to Lake Morena. During a break I extended one of my hiking poles too far and it came apart. I couldn't get it back together so I put it into my pack. I continued on just using the other pole.

There was a campground next to the lake that I could see in the distance. I had my map out because the Trail markings were confusing. Mouse caught up to me. He pointed to the right direction and we chatted as we headed to the campground. Mouse was in his twenties, had recently gotten out of the Navy, and was now going to college. He was hiking the Pacific Crest Trail during his summer break.

The campground had big shady trees, picnic tables, and water faucets, and we took a break. Mouse needed to get some things at the nearby store. I looked at my map and gave him directions. The store was four tenths of a mile away. Mouse took off as I was duct taping my hiking pole. I hadn't even finished doing this and Mouse was back. It was such a short period of time to walk eight tenths of a mile and get supplies that I asked if he had gotten lost. "Nope. I even had a couple of cups of coffee, got my caffeine, and I'm ready to go!" I took off as he was spreading peanut butter on a couple of tortillas. Being kind of competitive, I was going to show this guy he was dealing with an experienced hiker who could move pretty fast. Within minutes he was right on my tail. What? This couldn't be. He hadn't even started eating when I left.

He was a nice guy. A purist if there ever was one. Super enthusiastic. We passed an area next to a stream that had plants with large soft leaves. Mouse got excited. He picked off seven of the big leaves and put them in his pack. "Toilet paper" he said with satisfaction. He was an ultra-light hiker who had the smallest pack I had ever seen. It looked more like a day pack. His base weight, everything he carried in his pack minus food and water, weighed only seven and a half pounds. I'm a light weight backpacker and my base weight was double that. Mouse stayed right behind me and we chatted for a couple of hours. I was holding a good pace but was getting worn out. After a water break at a campground, I told Mouse to go ahead because I was slowing him down. I could see he was disappointed but he took off and that was the last I saw of him.

More than nine hundred people attempted to thru-hike the Pacific Crest Trail in 2012. Mouse started eleven days after the main group. By the time he finished there was only one hiker ahead of him. He finished in late July when the Trail in Oregon and Washington was still snow covered and treacherous. He averaged over thirty miles a day. It took him less than ninety days. I would finish more than two months later.

I was dragging for the rest of the day. I found a good camping spot next to the Trail but hidden from it by bushes. I could hear the sounds of a waterfall in a nearby canyon. I had not had much sleep the night before and had hiked most of the day at a fast pace. I was sleepy. After the sun went down it became cool enough that I was glad to get into my sleeping bag. I listened to birds settling in for the night and quickly was in a deep peaceful sleep. I woke the next morning to cheerfully chirping birds. It was cold. I decided to stay in my warm sleeping bag until the sun came over the mountain to warm me up. I rolled over and went back to sleep for another hour. It felt great.

In the desert most hikers would get up between 4:30 am and 5:00 am and start their hike just as it was getting light enough to see. The temperatures were cool before the sun came up and it was a pleasant time to hike. They would hike until 11:00 am and find a shady spot to wait out the 100 degree heat. At 4:00 pm they would continue hiking until dark. At home I usually get up at 5:30 am and it should have been easy to start early like the other hikers. For some reason I couldn't do it. Throughout my hike I was always listening to hikers walking by my tent in the morning, many times getting an hour or more head start. Being from the New Mexico desert and used to walking in the heat, I chose to hike throughout the day. When it got hot after 11:00 am I would slow down and drink a lot of water. That worked for me. I slept until I felt like getting up - usually between 7:00 am and 7:30 am and would be hiking an hour later. I liked my desert hiking system. It would have driven me nuts sitting in the shade for five hours, dealing with insects and doing nothing but shooting the bull, while I could have been making miles. If I averaged seventeen miles a day I would reach Kennedy Meadows, which was the start of the High Sierras, by the 19th of June. Any sooner and I would be dealing with snow in the high passes. I wasn't motivated to put in big miles at the start of my thru-hike, so sleeping until 7:00 am or later if I felt like it, was kind of a guilty pleasure.

The morning's hike was along the side of deep canyons. Eventually it led to the top of the mountain and to one of the things I loved about the Pacific Crest Trail - gorgeous views. As I was coming around a curve on the winding Trail a rattlesnake darted into the pathway inches in front of me. I immediately dug my toes into the dirt to keep from stepping on it and kicked a pile of dirt onto it. It was too close so I had to jump over it. Great! If the first rattlesnake was pissed, this one was Really Pissed! It turned toward me and rattled like crazy. I kept moving rapidly as I was glancing over my shoulder. I didn't know how fast a rattlesnake could move and I didn't want to find out. I had seen plenty of rattlesnakes over the years but never had one rattle at me. Now two in three days? What's going on here?

Eventually I reached Long Canyon, drank some refreshing water from Long Canyon Creek, and had my lunch under big, shady trees. The desert cactus and sage made way to pines and oaks as I got closer to Mt Laguna. Mt Laguna had a lodge, small store, and post office, but I didn't need any of these and continued hiking another mile before calling it a day. Once I was in my tent and reading about the area, I realized it was off limits to campers. It was 7:00 pm and I was tired. Screw it. After the Border Patrol incident I kept expecting a Forest Ranger to shine his light on my tent and order: "Out of the Tent!" I left early the next morning.

The Trail was wide and easy to hike. It was a hot day. I was hiking along the edge and sometimes deep into canyons. I was moving fast. I almost felt like I was getting my trail legs. In the afternoon I approached a pathway to a water source that was one half mile from the Trail. One part of my mind was telling me this was an especially hot day, I was drinking a lot of water, and needed to replenish. The other part was telling me it was a mile round trip, it wasn't supposed to be a good water source and I would have to treat it. The next water, where I planned to camp for the night, was only five miles and I still had two quarts, which was plenty. I walked past the turnoff.

The next five miles were hard, hot hiking with long climbs and a steep descent just before reaching Chariot Canyon Road. I was limiting my water intake and was thirsty. When I reached the dirt road, high in the mountains, it was 5:00 pm and I was down to less than a quart of water. The water source was dry! I had already hiked twenty miles and was extremely hot, tired, and thirsty. The next on-Trail water was four miles away at the Rodriguez Fire Tank. I had twenty-five ounces of water left. I looked at the map. The contour lines were close together and the path crossed the lines often. It wasn't going to be an easy four miles. I could make it before dark, but just barely. I was drained of energy. Could I make it in the 100 degree heat with only twenty-five ounces of water? What options did I have? I looked at the map again. There was a seasonal creek that crossed Chariot Canyon Road. It was 8/10ths of a mile north. There was a fire tank a half mile further.

I headed to the seasonal creek crossing. There wasn't enough water to create a puddle on the road. I had wasted a half an hour in the desert heat and had taken a few sips of desperately needed water. The fire tank HAD to have water. It looked old and unused. I opened the heavy lid on top. Dry as a bone! I was running out of options and getting thirstier by the minute. The interior of my mouth felt like cotton. I couldn't work up enough saliva to swallow. I headed back to the Trail.

Out of the corner of my eye, I caught a tiny glint in the creek bed. Could that be water? I had to find out. I bushwhacked thirty feet down the steep bank over thorny bushes and fallen trees. Once I reached the creek bed, I pushed through dense foliage until I reached the source of the glint. A flow of clear, cold water, about a yard in length, had made it to the surface. I couldn't believe my luck. I filled my water bottles and greedily drank two quarts on the spot. Water never tasted so good. I went from total dejection to jubilation in an instant.

A lot of the next six hundred miles was hot, hot, desert, and many times the water sources were few and far between. I had a set of Halfmile's maps for navigation. They showed the mileage in half mile increments from Mexico all the way to Canada. My brother, Doug, gave me a GPS for Christmas, bought Halfmile's maps for the GPS and downloaded them. The maps showed water sources, water alerts, fire detours, and a lot more. Sometimes the turn-off to a water source was not well marked and if you missed it you were screwed. Halfmile's maps were invaluable. Water became a precious commodity and making good decisions was essential. I and other hikes were obsessed with water and needed to be.

Roy Rogers was part of a singing group called The Sons Of The Pioneers. I was constantly singing and whistling one of his songs with feeling: "Cool, clear, water. Water….Water….Water…Cool, clear water."

The next morning I had absolutely no energy hiking the four miles to the Rodriguez Fire Tank. The hiking was difficult and I could tell it was going to be a very hot day. I made it to the fire tank at 11:00 am. There were bushes that provided a little shade. I filled and treated my four bottles of water with Aqua Mira drops. Other hikers joined me and it was fun chatting with them. One of them was Iron. He was enthusiastic almost to the point of being hyper. "I am pumped!" was a phrase he used over and over. After half an hour my water was purified. I should have cameled up by drinking as much of the purified water as I could, then filling up and purifying again. Big mistake. I had nine miles to get to the next water source at Scissors Crossing and thought I could easily make it with four quarts.

This was hot, hot, mountainous desert hiking. Within three miles I was out of the trees and in the hot desert sand. The sun was directly overhead and beating down. Its heat radiated off of the sand. It was over 100 degrees and I was sweating like crazy. I was extremely thirsty. It was so easy to drink half a quart of water at a time. I was starting to drag on the uphill climbs and still less than halfway there. All of a sudden I started to really feel the heat and feel my heart rate accelerate. I searched for some shade but there wasn't any for the next two miles. I finally came to a little cavern next to the Trail that was thirteen feet deep and ten feet wide.

I was out of the intense heat and could feel an immediate difference. There was a hot breeze through the cavern that wasn't soothing. I smoothed out an area on the dirt floor and lay down. My heart was racing. I closed my eyes and tried to relax. I fell asleep for half an hour. When I woke up I had some trail mix and drank a quart of water. I had a quart left to make it three miles. Fortunately the Trail was downhill and led out of the mountains onto a flat, level pathway to Scissors Crossing. I couldn't move any faster than one mile per hour. My heart was racing and I knew not to push it. I finally made it to the highway at Scissors Crossing and the gallons of water at the water cache. I chugged a quart of water without stopping. It tasted so good! I drank another quart. I had planned to continue on, but I was dirty, sweaty, and totally exhausted. That was about the most physically and emotionally drained I had been in my life.

I decided to hitch to Julian. Fortunately the third car picked me up. I was dropped off in front of the Julian Gold Rush Hotel Bed and Breakfast. There was a little sign that said: "PCT Hiker Discount". I was an extremely weary, dirty, smelly hiker with sweat rings of salt all over my shirt and shorts. As I went to the front desk to ask about prices I wasn't in the mood to have anyone look down their nose at me. The desk clerk greeted me with a cheerful smile. The price for a single was $65. I was given the keys to two rooms and I could pick the one I preferred. There was a room at the end of the hall, away from the traffic, that I chose. She handed me a plastic sack for my dirty clothes. The hotel cleaned my clothes for free. I headed to my room, took a much needed shower, and then a nap.

The hotel had been in continuous use since the 1890's. It had a great feel to it. The doors quietly creaked as they opened and closed and the room key was huge. It was a historic landmark and had been recently renovated, but it still had the feel of the 1890's. The interior was furnished from that time period and everything was spotless.

I dragged myself to the restaurant next door for dinner. The waitress took one look at me and left her pitcher of water on my table. I drank it all. I spent most of the time yawning and trying to stay awake. After dinner I headed back to my room, got into a big comfortable bed and slept for eleven straight hours.

The next morning I went down for breakfast. I told myself I would have their breakfast, which probably wouldn't be much, and then go across the street and have a real breakfast. Was I wrong! Breakfast was elegant. There was real china on the table and everything was immaculate. Breakfast started with granola and cream, a cup of yogurt, warm fresh baked bread and scones, a quiche, a basket of mixed fruit, and excellent coffee with a small pitcher of real cream. The owner came by my table a couple of times to see if I was liking my breakfast. I was. He was a perfectionist who took great pride in his hotel and his staff reflected that. This hotel exactly met my needs and did it with style. Check out time was noon. I went back to my room and slept for three more hours. By the time I left the hotel, I was clean, refreshed, recharged, and ready to hit the Trail.

When I reached Julian my hiking poles were shot. I threw them into the trash. Julian was a small town without an outfitter and I couldn't find hiking poles so I settled for a hiking stick. It came almost to my chin. I cut it down to the length of my hiking poles. As I used the hiking stick I started to like it. It gave me the balance and stability I needed. After a while I would automatically switch hands every fifteen to thirty seconds. In difficult areas I would use my right hand. Once an area smoothed out, I would switch back and forth. With a hiking stick I always had a free hand to swat flies (particularly those slow, biting, black flies) mosquitoes, gnats, wipe sweat off of my face, or eat trail mix. By the end of my hike I had big calluses between my thumb and forefinger and on the palms of both hands. I fell only a few times on my thru-hike but the hiking stick saved me from falls many times a day.

Scissors Crossing to Barrel Springs was a twenty-three mile waterless stretch through hot desert. I added an extra quart bottle of water. Fourteen miles into the hike there was a water cache at Third Gate. When I reached Third Gate there were over a hundred gallon jugs of water stashed under a big shady tree. I looked around for a dirt road or some way those jugs had been brought in. I couldn't find any. I learned later that many volunteers carried the jugs by hand over mountain trails to Third Gate. Thank you, Trail Angels.

In the desert, water caches were absolutely lifesavers. Trail Angels would go out of their way to keep gallon jugs of water filled for thru-hikers. Often caches were next to small, mountain, dirt roads. Sometimes there might be only a few jugs and other times there could be over one hundred. Trail Angels took on this responsibility and, throughout my hike, probably 95% of the time the water caches had water.

If you counted on the caches to have water and only carried enough water to get to a cache, you were a fool. You had to carry enough water to get to the next natural water source and you had to conserve your water until you made it to the cache, in case you found it empty. After miles of conserving water on an extremely hot day and carrying the extra water weight, it was a pleasure to get to the cache and find it had water. Then there was an orgy of water drinking. I could easily chug the first quart of water and keep drinking until I was completely full. Before I left I would top off my water bottles. Try chugging 32 ounces of water. If you are not thirsty, it's painful if not impossible. That might give you a feeling of the degree of thirst I felt in the desert.

The next nine miles from Third Gate to Barrel Springs was hot desert hiking in the San Felipe Mountains. The Trail was loose, sandy, dirt. At times, the downhill side had given way leaving it only a foot wide. It made for tricky and at times scary hiking. On one long stretch of uphill I felt like I could almost grab the hot, still, air. My shirt was soaked with sweat. As I came around a curve near the top of the mountain I walked into a shady area and was hit with a cool breeze. It went through both the front and back of my soaked shirt and felt wonderful.

I hiked late into the evening trying to find a place to put my tent. The only place I could find was on a ridge. The wind had gradually increased during the afternoon. By the time I was ready to put up the tent the wind was whipping. Small particles of sand were stinging my skin. As I grappled with the tent it was flapping wildly and would have taken off like a kite if given the opportunity. I finally pinned down each corner with heavy rocks and got the tent poles in. I staked it extra tight. For the next six hours the wind was incredible. Gusts would loudly slam into the tent, shaking the fabric violently. Fortunately the tent handled the wind beautifully.

The mountains gave way to huge, colorful, meadows the next day. Four miles before Warner Springs, California, I stopped at Eagle Rock. This was a rock formation that looked exactly like an eagle with its wings spread. I waited for half an hour for another hiker to show up so I could have my picture taken with the eagle in the background, but no luck. Finally, I took the first picture with my 27 shot disposable camera. My plan for this thru-hike was to take twenty-seven pictures of the highlights of the trip. It was a good plan, but poorly executed. For its protection, I had the camera tucked into a hard to reach area of the pack. Too often I didn't want to go through the hassle of taking things out of the pack to reach the camera.

I wanted to be in each shot. Sometimes I would be in a great location and no one was around to take the picture. I should have taken a picture at Campo at the start of the hike. I should have taken more in the gorgeous Sierra Nevada's. From the last two hundred miles of California, through Oregon and Washington, I was dodging wildfires. Many times I would be near a famous mountain and could barely see it through the smoke. I tried to save three pictures for the monument at the Canadian border. It was almost dark when I reached the border and no one was around to take the pictures. The next morning was bone chilling cold. I was freezing and needed to get moving to warm up. I skipped the pictures.

I took twenty pictures during my thru-hike. I had to take seven more when I returned home so I could develop the film. Of those twenty pictures there are only nine that are halfway decent. I'm sure my brother, Doug, who is a professional photographer, is shaking his head in disgust, disbelief, pity? "He can't take twenty-seven pictures in five months? On the Pacific Crest Trail?"

The Trail passed next to the tiny town of Warner Springs. It didn't have a store to resupply so I had a box of food and supplies sent to the Post Office. I had nine resupply boxes sent to me during my hike. I had enough food in each box to get to the next resupply town where I could buy my food at a grocery store. Each box had what I needed for that particular time of the hike: Toilet paper, Germex Hand Sanitizer, Chapstick, Petroleum Jelly, Neosporin, Walgreens SPF-50 Suntan Lotion, Ultrathon Insect Repellent, toothpaste, Band Aids, Duct Tape, socks, Brooks Cascadia 7 running shoes, and food. I planned on eating healthy during this hike and not cooking any meals. I relied heavily on a trail mix that I made and put into gallon plastic sacks. I figured I would eat about two pounds of food a day so each plastic sack weighed two pounds. I bought all my food at WalMart in one day and packaged it the same day. It was a pretty big undertaking. All the counter space in my kitchen was filled with boxes and bowls. My trail mix consisted of Shreaded Wheat Squares, and Shreaded Wheat Squares with Extra Fiber (not one of my better ideas), granola, raisins, dried apples, dried apricots, dried bananas, shelled sunflower seeds, mixed nuts, peanuts, and extra almonds. I filled a separate pint plastic bag with Wheat Thins and put one bag in each of the two pound sacks. By the time I reached Washington the Wheat Thins were stale. I started my hike with this trail mix. Within three days I realized two things: #1 – I only needed a pound of food a day. #2 - The trail mix was boring as hell.

When I reached Warner Springs, I was still carrying over five pounds of food. I only needed five days of food to get to the next resupply, so essentially, I didn't need the food from my mail drop. There was a hiker box in town where other hikers put food or supplies they didn't need and I added four of my sacks of trail mix to the box. This really worried me. I flat didn't like the food and I had eight more boxes with about eighty pounds of trail mix waiting for me down the trail. I will save you the suspense. As I got my hiker appetite the trail mix started tasting better. By the time I reached Oregon I was loving it. By that time two pounds of food a day was not enough and I was supplementing it with food I would buy in town.

Leaving Warner Springs, the next forty miles were some of the hottest I experienced. It was hot, dusty, sweaty, hiking with no shade and lots of climbing. I stopped for the night just short of Lost Valley Spring. I found a sandy spot surrounded by yuccas and ocotillo cactus to put my tent. High on a mountain with beautiful views it was the desert at its best. I hadn't seen another thru-hiker in five days and it was quiet and peaceful. I embraced the solitude. Before going to sleep, I lay on my back with my head out of the tent and gazed at a sky alive with stars. Without competition from city lights, the stars were brilliant. I had my hands clasped behind my head and felt completely calm and relaxed.

One of my most prized memories is of the many nights I slept alone. I didn't carry a phone, i-Pod, Kindle, or any other form of human distraction. On the Appalachian Trail I spent ninety percent of my nights around people - either camped near shelters or in shelters. On the Pacific Crest Trail I spent ninety percent of my nights camping alone. I loved it! The peacefulness, relaxation, and quiet, after a hard day of hiking bring back wonderful memories.

Once I was in my sleeping bag I would lay on my back and slowly and deeply inhale and exhale. I could feel any tension releasing from my body. I would be listening to the sounds of the night. Crickets were a constant. Birds make a low chirping sound just before calling it a night. I would hear them fluttering in the water. If I was lucky I would hear the soft hoot of an owl. If I was luckier I would hear coyotes making their mournful howls in the night. Sometimes there would be a family of coyotes nearby. They would start howling and stop at exactly the same time.

I tried to camp near flowing water. The sound was constant and relaxing. Often there were tones that sounded almost like a human voice. I would listen closely before realizing it was just the water.

Ponderosa pines were my favorite trees. Camped underneath, I would smell their delicate pine fragrance and listen to the soothing sound of the breeze through their branches.

I had some of the best quality sleeps of my life on the Pacific Crest Trail. As a child I remember reading about Huckleberry Finn floating down the Mississippi River on a raft on a star filled night. It sounded carefree and fun. Sometimes, lying on my back and gazing at a sky full of stars, it felt like I didn't have a care in the world.

Halfmile's maps had little tent symbols for places to camp. They were usually near water and had level places to put a tent. Hikers would plan to meet at one of these designated camping areas at the end of the day. Sometimes they would hike well into the night to get there. They could socialize and it made them feel secure.

I rarely stopped at a destination. I always set a goal for that particular day. If I wanted to put in big miles and daylight lasted until 8:30 pm, my goal for finding a camp site was 8:00 pm. At times I would be on the side of a mountain and it would be almost dark before I found a place to put my tent but I rarely had to hike into the night. I looked for an area where the dirt had been smoothed out and was fairly level. Ideally it would be near a spring or stream. I camped in a variety of locations – mountaintops, valleys, next to waterfalls, streams, rivers, gorges, surrounded by lava. There were times when a perfect location would show up and it would only be 5:00 pm. Almost always I would continue on.

I filled my water bottles in the morning at Lost Valley Spring. The next natural water was seventeen miles away. The next potential water was a cache or a water tank in seven miles. The cache was empty. I knew I needed water so I headed .2 miles north on a little dirt road to the water tank that belonged to Mike Herrera. He owned a ranch that looked like the only ranch for miles in any direction. This generous man let hikers take water from his water tank. When I reached the tank, I turned on the spigot and no water came out. I needed water badly so I headed down to the house. He wasn't home but he had a shady porch with chairs for hikers to relax. A hose was connected to the house and I tried that. Still no water. He had a ten gallon tub of water in the shade for hikers. There were dead flies and other things floating on top. I needed water. I put my water bottles into the tub and filled them. I added the Aqua Mira drops and shook each bottle thoroughly. I gave the drops a full hour instead of half an hour to do their magic. The water had a powerful rubbery taste. I didn't care. I needed the water.

The Paradise View Cafe was in twenty-five more miles. All hikers looked forward to stopping there. I was sick of my trail mix which was about all I had eaten since starting my hike. Paradise View Cafe was said to have hiker portions and good food. I picked up my pace. This section was completely desert with lots of sand, sage, mesquite, and cactus. There were beautiful rock formations with tiny seeps of water that were barely enough for a lizard. When I took rest breaks, little hummingbirds would come within a yard of my nose, hover for a couple of seconds and dart off. It was fun and happened all the time. I wore a bright red shirt. Maybe that was the attraction.

There were places where the Trail had broken down that were only about a foot wide. They were on the side of the mountain, sometimes with long steep drop-offs. The Pacific Crest Trail more so than the Appalachian Trail had pathways high on the sides of mountains where if you slipped and fell over the side, you were going to die. When I reached one of these areas I would look over the edge and gasp. I would make sure my hiking stick was firmly planted and slowly work my way over loose rocks, trying to stay as far away from the edge as possible. After I made it through I would let the air out in a long exhale and my first thought was: "That was not fun!" My second thought was: "You know, it kind of was, though." I can see how adrenaline junkies get that way.

The next ten miles from Herrera's Ranch to Tule Spring was hot hiking. I had a big, floppy shade hat for protection from the constant sun and was glad to have it. There were two clothing approaches to hiking in the desert. I wore black shorts and a red short sleeved shirt. Other hikers wore long pants and long sleeved light colored shirts. I don't know how they could stand being covered that much in the heat of the day but they were in the majority. I would say the breakdown was 60% long pants, long sleeved shirts to 40% shorts and short sleeved shirts.

I loaded up with water at Tule Spring for the fourteen miles to the Paradise View Cafe. I made it there by noon the next day. It felt good sitting in the air conditioned café. I ordered the beef and bean burrito. When the burrito arrived it completely covered a large plate. It was delicious. When I finished, I ordered the homemade apple pie with two scoops of vanilla ice cream. Heavenly! I left a full, happy, hiker. I was so full I was drowsy on the mile walk from the cafe back to the Trail. I just wanted to find a shady tree, curl up, and take a nap. Finally the food energy kicked in and I was really moving the rest of the day.

I kept waiting to see another thru-hiker. I hadn't seen one on the Trail for over one hundred miles. Many thru-hikers started their hike after the annual Pacific Crest Trail "Kick Off". It was held on April 28th and 29th at the Lake Morena campground. It was a popular event and the big campground was completely full. The Kick Off was a way for current PCT thru-hikers to get to know one another and former thru-hikers to share their experience. There was free food, vendors with the latest light weight gear, water reports for the desert, and seminars on topics such as bears. There were over nine hundred hikers attempting a thru-hike of the Pacific Crest Trail in 2012. A normal year would be closer to five hundred. Hikers who started right after the Kick Off were known as the "Herd". I started my hike on the 9th of May. I didn't want to get to the High Sierras too early and run into snow, and I didn't want to be part of the Herd. May 9th turned out to be a good start date, but even for me, one hundred miles without seeing another thru-hiker on the Trail was a bit much.

I was heading into the San Jacinto Mountains. The desert gradually gave way to pine, oak, and cedar forests and the mountains became higher. Water sources were still scarce and this was hard hiking. I was drinking a lot of water. Tunnel Spring was only eight miles from the Paradise View Cafe where I topped off my water before I left, but I was already almost out. Tunnel Spring was three-tenths of a mile steeply downhill from the Trail and I was dreading coming back up with five quarts of water. The water had a sulfur taste but I needed it badly.

The San Jacinto Mountains were beautiful and a welcome change from the desert, but they were brutal. I was feeling proud of myself. I was handling the difficult hiking well. I wasn't too tired and still had energy to spare. I reached an intersection high in the mountains and there was a thru-hiker taking a break. It was the first thru-hiker I had seen in over a hundred miles. Then another one showed up. It was fun talking to them but I lost my focus. When I started hiking again I took the wrong turn at the trail junction. I headed down the Forbes Ranch Trail instead of the PCT. There was a green water tank way in the distance that I eventually passed as I descended, then it became way in the distance in the other direction. Finally, I hit the trailhead. There were no signs mentioning the PCT. I had been traveling downhill for three miles. I looked at my map and immediately found my error. Now I had to hike steeply uphill, in the heat of the day, for three miles just to get back to the PCT. I was Pissed! That took a lot out of me both physically and emotionally. When I reached the Trail again, the other hikers had taken off so I didn't have to look like a complete idiot in front of them. There was a good sized climb to further sap my energy. Just before dark I made it to the top of the mountain and found a great place to camp. The lights of Palm Springs, California were glowing in the distance. I hiked eighteen hard miles but could only count twelve of them. I was tired and frustrated.

The next day I had eleven miles to get to Saddle Junction and take the Devil's Slide Trail down to Idyllwild, California and a resupply. I had no energy at all. I was hiking in the beautiful San Jacinto Mountains and was deep into my misery. This was a Sunday and only fifty miles from the Los Angeles area. The Trail was teeming with happy hikers. I wanted to wallow in self-pity but being around so many cheerful hikers was making it difficult.

I made it to Idyllwild and walked through a maze of streets before finally finding the center of town. I knew I had to take another unplanned motel break. I was beat. I checked in at the Idyllwild Inn. I was so tired my voice was no more than a croak as I was talking to the desk clerk. I took a long, hot, shower and washed off days of dirt. The motel cleaned my funky clothes for free. I shopped for groceries, brought them back to my room, and headed to Grandma's Deli. I ordered a parmesan sandwich and a chicken sandwich and they were huge. In normal circumstances I probably couldn't have finished one of them. I finished both and was stuffed. I headed back to the motel room. It was 8:00 pm. I could barely keep my eyes open. I slept until 7:00 the next morning. The owner of the hiker friendly motel gave me a ride to the trailhead which saved a three mile hike. It was like night and day. I went from total dejection coming off the Trail to raring to go when he dropped me off. The two cups of coffee with cream and sugar didn't hurt either.

This was a great day for hiking in one of the prettiest areas on the Pacific Crest Trail. It was a healthy, vibrant, forest. After the desert, it was a pleasure to drink cold mountain water right from a stream and have another stream show up a mile later.

That evening I found a camping spot high on the mountain and watched the setting sun turn beautiful shades of red.

I started early the next morning because I knew I had a hot hike ahead of me. I would be hiking from Fuller Ridge, high in the mountains, all the way to the desert floor. There were places hikers talked about around campfires. This was one of them. Many hikers, over the years, quit at Fuller Ridge.

Sometimes on my Halfmile maps I would make notations. On top of the Fuller Ridge map I wrote: "Hot, exposed, tricky, steep. Downhill for hours. Started with five quarts of water. Could have used ten." From Fuller Ridge to the next water source which was a water fountain on the desert floor, I had to hike fifteen miles.

"Hot." The heat started early, even high on the mountain, and increased with each mile downhill. I loaded my skin with Shade 50 suntan lotion but the sun beating down on my arms was almost painful.

"Exposed." There were few areas to find shade. Once in a while there was a huge boulder. The ground was so worn in its shaded area, you could see that every hiker had taken refuge from the intense heat.

'Tricky." It was an enormous task just for trail maintainers to get half way up this steep trail in the heat. Most of the Trail on the upper half was not maintained. Bushes were covering parts of the Trail and I had to push my way through them. At times I couldn't see where I was placing my feet and the pathway was sandy and uneven. I was depending on my hiking stick to stay upright. In places, the sides of the Trail were not shored up and parts of the pathway had crumbled down the mountain. It was tricky hiking. Miles and miles of tricky hiking.

"Steep." Miles and miles of steep, too. Often on a loose, sandy, pathway.

"Downhill for hours." It was fifteen miles of winding downhill. At two miles per hour, that was over seven hours of hiking and it just got hotter and hotter. Every hiker talked about passing buzzing bees near the bottom. There was a little cave created by boulders to the right of the Trail. I could hear the buzzing before I saw the bees. They were swarming around the entrance and into the pathway. There was no way around them so I shot by as fast as I could, brushing some of them.

"Started with five quarts of water. Could have used ten." I knew I was going to need all five quarts so I paced myself to a quart every two hours. I felt really thirsty the whole time. It was a relief to make it to the desert floor and drink from the water fountain.

At the water fountain I met two section hikers sprawled in the shade of a boulder. We had a five mile walk over a hot paved road and hot desert sand before reaching our destination. Lightweight caught up to us as we were getting ready to leave. Lightweight was the first person I met who I would see again and again all the way to Washington. He had just graduated from college and was doing this hike before entering the workforce. We didn't hike at the same speed. He was much faster but he loved his zeros. He was very social and could tell a good story. Towns that I would stop for a resupply and head out the same day, Lightweight would stay for a day...or two...or three....or four. For hundreds of miles he seemed to be a couple of days ahead of me or a couple of days behind me. It was always a pleasure to bump into him on the Trail. He was having a great time and fun to be around.

Our destination was Ziggy and the Bear's. They were a retired couple who let hikers stay in their backyard for the night. Their yard had a high white fence, which was necessary, because the little town where they lived had the second highest continuous wind velocity in the United States. There was a wind farm nearby. I was thinking of stopping at Ziggy and the Bear's, taking a short break, and heading out to find a place to camp but the wind was ferocious. They had a big tent attached to the back of their home that helped protect us from the wind. I opted to spend the night. I didn't even want to try putting my tent up in that wind. Windblown hikers kept coming in and by the time the last hiker arrived there were fourteen of us. We were treated to an Epsom Salt footbath. The water was so hot I could barely keep my feet in the tub for more than a few seconds. I had an open blister on my right foot that stung when it hit the salty water. After a while I was able to keep my feet in the water and it felt great. The water in my little tub was black by the time I finished. Ziggy brought out fresh salad for all of us and there were apples, oranges, chips and dips, cookies, and three choices of ice cream for dessert. There were pieces of carpet to sleep on. Most of the hikers opted to sleep in the tent and were packed in like sardines. I decided to sleep on the sandy ground away from the tent and was whipped by the sand and gusty wind all night long. I don't think anyone got much sleep and the loudly flapping tent didn't help. The next morning at 5:30, Ziggy brought out cereals and milk with fresh fruit. There was coffee, too. It was a good way to start the morning. There was a donation jar and I put in a twenty dollar bill.

I had seen pictures of wind turbines in Yogi's PCT Handbook and was looking forward to seeing one. Yogi's PCT Handbooks (Planning Guide) and (Trail Tips and Town Guide) were invaluable for planning my hike. Just about every hiker used them. Yogi thru-hiked the PCT three times and drew on her experiences. The "Planning Guide" covered everything you would want to know before starting a thru-hike of the PCT: Pre-hike considerations (Permits, maps, ideal start and finish dates, hiking alone or with others, the cost of a thru-hike, conditioning before a thru-hike) Ultralight Hiking, Gear, Clothing, Footwear, Personal Care, The Desert, The Sierras, Trail Towns, Mail drops, Resupply, and much more. On each subject, she gave her opinion and the opinions of other PCT thru-hikers. She had up to twenty hikers who would contribute on any given topic. This gave me a variety of opinions on a subject, such as boots vs. trail runners and was very helpful.

Her "Trail Tips and Town Guide" gave the water sources along the PCT and how to get to them. She rated a lot of them and gave other hiker's evaluations. When I was planning my hike from November 2011 to May 2012, I circled the water sources listed on Halfmile's maps and used Yogi's evaluations. I would put "Good Water" or "Bad Water" and sometimes even "Skanky Water". It was a lot of work but I did this for all 2,660 miles of the PCT. I would plan my day to hit the good water sources. Sometimes I would even carry extra water to get to the good sources. I purified my water only eight times and didn't get giardia. Many hikers came down with giardia in 2012 and many of them filtered religiously. I think they put too much faith in their filtering systems and often filtered "skanky" water.

The "Town Guide" section listed each town along the Trail and how to get to it. It told the times the Post Office was open and if there were grocery stores, outfitters, laundry, phones, ATM's, and internet service. She had a list of the motels with their price range and which were hiker friendly. She listed the restaurants with other hiker's evaluations of the food quality. She had a map of each town that showed where to find each restaurant, motel, grocery store, outfitter, and the Post Office. Phone numbers were included and often when hikers reached a road leading into town they would call one of the motels and the owner would pick them up. Hikers tore out the small pages of the "Trail Tips and Town Guide" and put them in baggies. Yogi's Handbooks were excellent. Hikers were always quoting Yogi: "Yogi says that this motel….."

The next day was one of the most enjoyable of my hike. I think this was the day I realized that, barring injury, nothing was going to keep me from completing my thru-hike. It was a punishing day through an area that had a well-deserved reputation for being tough. I had eaten a lot of food at Ziggy and the Bear's and had energy to spare. The morning started with a gradual climb through a sandy area. There were wind turbines close to the Trail. It was a windy morning and their huge blades were creaking and humming.

This was true desert hiking. There were few trees and the ground was mainly sand with occasional clumps of dry, brown, grass. The area was filled with long, deep, canyons. Often I could see the Trail far in the distance and the switchbacks that were going to take me to the bottom of a canyon and the switchbacks that were going to take me up the other side. On top were areas that were fairly flat for miles where I was completely exposed to the hot sun. The word HOT was constantly being battered around in my mind. A steep, winding, pathway led down to the Whitewater River. Its water was cold and refreshing. I drank a lot. The river had a wide bed which was sandy and difficult to navigate. Hiker's footprints headed in all directions and it was confusing trying to figure out where the Trail continued on the other side. Once I found it I was immediately hiking through more canyons, some of them deep and steep. One of them was a box canyon that curved and climbed and when I neared the top I looked back to see if there were any hikers behind me. Three hikers were heading my way and looked like little ants far in the distance.

Sixteen miles into the day's hike I took a break at Mission Creek. The smoothly flowing water had been so exposed to the hot sun that it was warm when I drank it. The Trail continued to wind up and down more canyons. There were no roads anywhere. The only way out was on foot or horseback. It was dry, dusty, sandy, hot, brown, desert hiking for mile after mile.

I made it to my camping spot by 7:00 in the evening. I was tired. I had put in twenty-five miles of hard hiking. Only one of the fourteen hikers who started in the morning at Ziggy and the Bear's made it to the campsite and he came in an hour later. I finally had my trail legs and it felt great! Here are my notes on Halfmile's map for this area: "Beautiful, extremely hot, twenty-five mile desert hiking. Plenty of water. Drank ten quarts during the day. Pissed once. Dark yellow."

I was wondering if I would be tired the next morning after the all-out twenty-five mile day. I felt good and ready to go. I filled up with water from the nearby stream and set out early in the morning. The desert gave way to forests of fragrant pines and cedars but the hiking was difficult. I meant to fill my water bottles at Mission Springs Trail Camp, four miles into the hike, but wasn't paying attention and passed right by. There was a lot of climbing. As the day progressed it got hotter. For some idiotic reason, I hadn't planned very well for this day. I didn't even know where the next water source was and was drinking my water freely. Eventually I looked at my map. Yikes! I had ten more miles to go and less than a quart of water left. These were steep mountains. My next water source was a water cache and the one after that was four miles further. If the cache was empty I would have to hike fourteen miles on less than a quart of water on the steep uphill Trail in the heat of the day. I think more out of anxiety than anything else, I picked up my pace. I was moving uphill at over three miles an hour and continued at that pace until I reached the cache three hours later. I was down to four ounces of water. The water cache was full. I felt like a lucky fool, though. From then to the end of my hike I looked at the water sources and planned my hike better at the start of each day.

As I continued my hike I passed a bunch of cages. They looked abandoned to me. I may have seen the faint outline of a lion but I wasn't sure. Tipi Hedron, the actress who starred in 'The Birds", an Alfred Hitchcock film, built these cages to take care of retired film stunt animals. There were supposed to be lions and tigers and bears. When I talked with another hiker a half an hour later he asked if I had seen all the animals and described them. We had to have gone over the same pathway. It left me scratching my head.

Further up the Trail I caught up to Lightweight who was taking a break. Trail Angels had carried a big sofa from the road to the Trail and left sodas, apples, and oranges. It felt great to sit on the soft sofa with a coke in one hand and a juicy apple in the other. There was a notebook where hikers thanked the Trail Angels. On the Appalachian Trail hikers communicated through shelter journals. On the PCT you kept track of other hikers by reading the registers. There was almost always a notebook with a pen next to trail magic. The registers were sometimes at post offices, motels, restaurants, or entering national forests. Hikers would put their name, the date, and a short message. You could tell which hikers were ahead of you and if they were leaving you in the dust.

I camped under a huge cedar tree that night. I could see the headlights of cars and trucks on the distant freeway and hear the trucks straining on the uphill grade. The wind picked up in the night and I had my fingers crossed a branch wouldn't break and fall on my tent.

The next day started off warm. In the afternoon, clouds began to develop. As the day wore on they started getting darker. I was heading to the top of the mountain and could feel the temperature getting colder. I added my windbreaker. By 6:00 pm I had on my long sleeved shirt, rain jacket, gloves, and balaclava. I was losing body heat even with all of this on so I picked up my pace to try to generate more body heat. That wasn't working and I knew I had to get out of the cold pretty quickly. I found a place to put my tent on the edge of Van Dusen Canyon. My hands were cold even with the gloves on. I needed to get into the tent and into my twenty degree sleeping bag. It worked. I started to gradually warm up. I ate a lot of trail mix to help stay warm in the night. Around 8:00 pm the wind picked up. I was near the top of the mountain and Van Dusen Canyon went all the way down to Big Bear City, three miles in the distance. By 10:00 pm the wind was alarming. I would hear a wind gust come barreling up the canyon. The sound would become louder and louder so that by the time it hit the tent it sounded like a freight train – WHOOOM! For hours the gusts kept hitting the tent. I was lucky to have a good tent. It was cold in the night. The wind chill had to have been in the teens. I had gone past the limits of my sleeping bag and was scrunched up in a little ball trying to stay warm. I didn't get much sleep. In the night I heard something hitting my tent. I thought it was rain. When I opened the tent the next morning, it was covered with snow. The wind was still blowing, it was cold, and I was groggy from lack of sleep. I stayed in my sleeping bag for another three hours and slept most of that time. I was in no hurry to get started. The sun stayed mainly behind the clouds for most of the day and it was cold and windy. I had on all of my warm clothes. My balaclava was covering my face and nose with just my eyes showing, and I was cold. I didn't take off my balaclava or start shedding jackets until after 2:00 pm. To go from blazing hot on the 24th of May to snow on May 25th, go figure.

I spent a lot of May 26th hiking through a burned area. It was sad to go from lush, healthy, forest, to seeing the same type of trees and underbrush all blackened and dead. The fire in this area happened in 2007. A ground cover of plants and flowers was beginning to take hold. One of the first plants to show up after a fire was the Poodle Dog Bush. It was hardy and was everywhere. It could grow up to five feet high, had purple flowers, and a pungent, unpleasant, smell. I could always tell when I was getting near one. Hikers, trail maintainers, forest rangers, guidebooks, Halfmile, and others, had warnings about the Poodle Dog Bush. It was supposed to be worse than poison ivy and poison oak. Sometimes there were long road walks because the Trail hadn't been maintained and there was too much Poodle Dog Bush next to the Trail. A lot of hikers had a real fear of it and would worry if they brushed against it. I brushed against it a lot. Sometimes the pathway was thick with it and I couldn't avoid it. After a while I wouldn't take the detours and stayed on the pathway. There were so many warnings it became a joke to some of us. On the Trail there would be a rock holding down a handwritten note: "Poodle Dog Bush ahead." "Not the Poodle Dog Bush!"

Six miles into the next day's hike I hit the 14.2 mile Deep Creek Detour. Halfmile's maps showed that it bypassed 15.7 miles of the PCT damaged by winter storms in December 2010. The storms caused landslides across steep sections of the Trail and damaged several bridges. The regular PCT followed Deep Creek all 15.7 miles and hikers described it as a beautiful, fun hike, with a hot spring to soak in. I didn't learn until later a lot of work had been done since the storm and many hikers were using the regular Trail instead of the detour. I was kind of pissed, then I thought about it, and it was definitely a memorable day. I even had to grudgingly admit I enjoyed it. It was Sunday May 27th, the day before Memorial Day. The detour was through hot, exposed, desert. It was within twenty miles of San Bernardino, California which is near Los Angeles. There were almost no trees. The first seven miles of the detour was on a climbing dirt road so rutted and bumpy it could only be used by off road vehicles. On curves, the road was banked at steep angles. There was tons of dust. Any time it crossed a stream, there were huge mud puddles. I picked the day of the annual off road vehicle rally to hike it. The mood was festive. It was noisy. Mufflers were optional. It felt like a thousand ATV's, dirt bikes, dune buggies, hummers, jeeps, and anything that was four wheel drive, passed me. It was probably a couple of hundred but it felt like a thousand.

The awning covered golf carts were my favorites. Each one had a music system that was blaring. The people were laid back, putting along at less than ten miles an hour, drinking their favorite beverage. A man and his wife gave me a big smile and a YEE HAW as they sedately putted by. It made me laugh. I think if I had been jogging I would have passed them. The dirt bikers were another story. They would shoot by spewing dirt and dust. If there were puddles in the road, the golf carts would delicately go through them or around them if they could. The dirt bikers barreled straight through shooting water and mud everywhere. It was hard, hot, hiking. I ate a lot of dust those three and a half hours. I finally made it to Highway 173 and followed it for seven miles downhill along the side of a mountain. It felt good to stride out. I was hiking over four miles an hour. I could see the PCT way on the other side of the deep canyon. I spent the last two miles of the day climbing in an area that was a combination of desert and forest. I set up my tent on a bluff overlooking the Mojave River Forks Reservoir. When it became dark I could see the lights of towns far in the distance.

The next day was out of the ordinary and enjoyable, too. It started with eight miles of great hiking along the side of a mountain. The views to the northwest were limitless. I could see farms, ranches, faraway towns, and possibly even Barstow, California.

I passed a cute jogger heading in the opposite direction. She was followed by her bulldog who had a "life is good" look on his face. Twenty yards later there was a huge dump, dead center on the Trail. I eventually passed a dam which created the Silverwood Lake State Recreation Area. This was Memorial Day and the lake was full of motorboats. The Trail stayed fairly close to the big lake for the next five miles.

Every piece of sandy beach had been staked out. Boats would land on the beach and people would get out and set up a picnic. All the parking lots next to the campgrounds and picnic areas were full. Police officers were turning cars away. Cars were parked along the sides of the highway for over a mile. Hordes of people rolling ice chests and carrying umbrellas headed down the pathways from the highway to the picnic areas. It was noisy and festive. Lots of people were swimming and the blue water looked inviting. I needed to get some water from the campground because it was hot and I was drinking a lot. The next water was in six miles of uphill desert hiking. I didn't want to be close to that many loud, extroverted, people and decided to skip getting the water and take my chances. By the fifth mile I was regretting my decision. I finally made it to a small stream. I was so hot that I filled my hat with iced cold water and put it on my head. After the initial shock it felt great. The rest of the day was hot, difficult, desert hiking and after searching for a long time I found a spot for my tent next to a small stream. I was one mile from Interstate 15 and the much anticipated McDonalds Restaurant.

I was awakened the next morning by a coyote giving me fits. It stayed about one hundred feet away and howled and yipped for at least a half an hour. It was clearly distressed so I quickly packed up and headed out. You would think something as unimpressive as having breakfast at McDonalds would be no big deal. Every hiker I talked to within three days of reaching McDonalds mentioned how much they were looking forward to it. I was no exception. I was up early the next morning in anticipation and had a spring in my step. I had their biggest breakfast of sausage, scrambled eggs, two pancakes, two pieces of toast, and hash browns, plus the McSkillet breakfast burrito. It's hard to describe how good it tasted after days of trail mix. The only time I had caffeine was during town stops and occasionally a coke when I came upon trail magic. Having a big cup of coffee with extra cream and sugar was a luxury. Leaving McDonalds, I was charged and ready to kick some butt! I hiked twenty-four extremely hard miles that day.

I met Sprinkles as he was heading out of McDonalds. We only hiked together for a couple of hours but those hours were memorable. He was in his late twenties. He lived in California and had hiked most of the PCT in sections. He was doing a thru-hike for the first time and his knowledge of the PCT was impressive. The area we were hiking was hot, dry, desert, full of cactus, chaparral, and yucca trees. He was a lightweight backpacker who had a tiny tarp tent which he hardly ever used. He said he didn't enjoy the camping experience and preferred to cowboy camp under the stars. I would bet he used his tarp tent less than ten times the whole length of the PCT. He was super fit and even though I had just eaten at McDonalds and had energy to spare, I was moving fast and having a hard time keeping up with him. Another thru-hiker had just given him the trail name Sprinkles and he wasn't sure if he wanted to keep it. He didn't think it sounded masculine enough. I told him it had kind of a happy innocence to it. I noticed from register entries that he kept it. I was getting worn out trying to keep up with him. When we reached a ridge after a long climb, I told him I would catch up to him later – which surprisingly, I did. Two miles later there was a water cache and Sprinkles was sitting on a lawn chair enjoying a lime flavored mineral water. I joined him. (I have Halfmile's map of this section as I am writing this and I just noticed we were sitting right on the San Andreas – earthquake - Rift.) I was really thirsty. I topped off my water bottles and cameled up almost to the point of being uncomfortable. Good decision. The rest of the day was continuous uphill. Some other hikers joined us and I took off while Sprinkles stayed behind to visit. As I approached the first mountain I could see another mountain far in the distance and what looked like the outline of the Trail way at the top. This happened over and over. It could be disheartening seeing how far I had to hike uphill on a very hot day but I felt great and just went full out. Other than a couple of small breaks, I kept the pace until I reached my destination which was a campground two miles before Highway 2 that led to Wrightwood, California. I set up my tent and just as I was finishing, Sprinkles reached the campground and came over: "You are a fast hiker, Jim." I can't remember how I handled the compliment, but coming from Sprinkles, it meant a lot. I didn't see Sprinkles again until Etna, California just before Oregon. He could have hiked much faster but sometimes he would hike with a group or individuals which would slow him down. After Etna he started hiking by himself. By the time he finished the PCT he was two weeks ahead of me - easily three hundred miles.

The first car that came by the next morning picked me up and the driver dropped me off at the Pines Motel in Wrightwood. It's amazing how much people will tell about themselves on a twenty minute ride. I had been putting in high mileage days and was looking forward to some rest. I checked in at the Pines Motel. I think I should have checked the room beforehand. It was pretty rickety. The motel had been there for many years and there had been few upgrades in that time. The faucets creaked and squeaked and the toilet needed two flushes. There was a wooden pallet to stand on in the tiny shower and I was thinking athlete's foot as I was showering. The room cost the same as the great bed and breakfast in Julian.

I was kind of grumbling until I got acquainted with the owner. He was a tiny Korean man whose English was hard to understand. I don't think anyone else worked there. He cleaned the rooms, checked people in and out, and did the laundry, including my clothes, for free. Since there wasn't a phone in my room he let me use his phone to call my sister, Johanna, my brother, Doug, my aunt, Nancy, and my neighbor, Joyce, who was taking care of my dog, Fred. I loved his upbeat, friendly, attitude. He left me with a pleasant memory. My room was clean, the bed was comfortable, and after resupplying and having two excellent burritos at the deli, I came back to the room and slept like a baby.

The library was next to the motel and had a computer. The next morning I emailed Doug. I hadn't been able to get my GPS to work properly. Halfmile's waypoints wouldn't show up. The first day of my hike the waypoints showed up but from then on I couldn't access them. I thought that somehow I had erased them. I was very frustrated and asked Doug if he could put a section of Halfmiles maps on his GPS and send his GPS to me in Mojave, California. Once I reached Mojave I would send him my GPS and see if he could fix it. My GPS was still useful. It showed the miles I hiked which helped keep me oriented on the map but I wanted the waypoints.

My time on the computer was running short and people were waiting to use it so I wasn't able to wait for a response. Before heading back to the Trail I had two more burritos. Delicious!

Another easy hitch and another person about my age picked me up. That happened quit a few times. The first question usually was: "Wow! That's a long hike. Why are you doing this?" I had some practice answering that. (Thank you, Johanna.)

My goal for the day was to climb Mt. Baden Powell and end on the other side at Little Jimmy Campground. By 5:00 pm I was only half way to the top. I walked by a camping spot under huge ponderosa pine trees with their wonderful vanilla/pine fragrance. It was a hot day and the shade made it instantly cooler. The views were limitless and stupendous. I still had three more hours I could hike but this was too good to pass up. I set up my tent on a soft mat of pine needles and spent some leisurely time exploring the area. There were old, gnarled, bristlecone pines only a few yards from my tent. I could only imagine the snows, wind, ice, rain, and fires they had endured for hundreds of years. When I returned to my tent, I tried one last time to get my GPS working. I went through everything and finally came across a section called "extras". There they were - the PCT waypoints for California, Oregon, and Washington. I clicked on California and the compass arrow pointed to the nearest waypoint, complete with distance and time to get there. It was only a quarter of a mile away and I headed to it. It worked beautifully. I was elated. There were good vibrations from this campsite. A gentle breeze was flowing through the pines creating a soothing sound. An owl kept me company during parts of the night with its simple, quiet: Hoot.........Hoot.

I had asked Doug to program his GPS and send it to Mojave. I needed to let him know my GPS was working before he went to all that extra effort. The nearest phone was at the Acton KOA Campground, seventy miles away. For the next three days I was a motivated hiker. Leaving my peaceful campsite, I headed up Mt. Baden Powell. Just before reaching the summit I stopped next to a huge bristlecone pine. There was a sign dedicating the 1,500 year old tree to the founder of the Boy Scouts of

America - the Wally Waldron Tree. Birdie showed up and took my picture. A few minutes later I was on top of Mt. Baden Powell with 360 degree views. There was a monument to the founder of the Boy Scouts - Lord Robert Baden-Powell. I hiked with Birdie the next three hours. She was in her forties and kept a good pace. We followed a road walking detour to protect the Mountain Yellow-legged Frog and ended up in a large campground. Birdie found a couple of birdwatchers to talk to and the last I saw her she was imitating the hoot of an owl to an appreciative audience.

I hiked thirty-one miles the next day. This was hot, rugged, desert hiking. A couple of fire stations next to the Trail provided much needed water. I passed areas that had been badly burned and the Trail was covered with ash. By the end of the day I was covered with soot. I caught up with Hannah, Caveman, Tripod, and Mark just before dark. We were all headed to a campsite listed on Halfmile's map. There had been a recent fire in the area and the campsite no longer existed. We kept going trying to find a flat spot. By the time we found a fairly level spot we were using our headlamps. Hanna, Caveman, Tripod, and Mark were camped in a wide area next to the Trail. I was camped on a little dirt road next to the Trail. I put my tent over motorcycle tracks and wondered what I was going to do if a motorcycle came roaring around the corner early the next morning. We chatted as we set up our tents and prepared our food. Mark had recently talked with his wife on the phone while he was in Wrightwood. He said she didn't understand why he was hiking the Pacific Crest Trail. He asked me if I had an answer for her. I had just hiked thirty-one miles. I was exhausted and my answer was uninspired: "I don't know."

He wasn't impressed. The next morning there was a long climb through a pine forest to the top of a mountain. I stopped to take a break. I was in a big meadow full of thick green grass that was gently flowing in the breeze. A hummingbird was flitting around sipping nectar. There were panoramic views. Hannah, Caveman, and Mark, caught up to me and stopped for a break. We were completely relaxed as we ate our pop tarts and trail bars. I said to Mark: "This is why I'm hiking. Is there anything more beautiful? When we woke up this morning did you hear all the birds singing? We just climbed a mountain for two solid hours with backpacks and we aren't even breathing hard. Have you ever been in better condition in your life? I feel lucky to be out here." There were nods of agreement.

Within a couple of miles we were back into, gnarly, mountainous, desert hiking on one of the hottest days yet. I reached the Acton KOA Campground at 4:00 pm after a twenty-one mile day. The other hikers were younger and faster and most of them were already in the swimming pool. I called Doug immediately and breathed a huge sigh of relief when he told me he was just getting ready to program his GPS.

Ten miles up the Trail was the resupply town of Agua Dulce. Hiking high on the mountain I would see a little town far in the distance, think it was Agua Dulce, and the Trail would pass it by. This happened a couple of times until I reached Vasques Rock County Park which was right next to Agua Dulce. It was full of narrow desert canyons with small caves and uniquely shaped, colorful, rock formations. A stream flowed through the park and was lined with mesquite, willow, and cottonwood trees. A Star Trek episode was filmed there and at one time it was the hideout of a notorious Mexican bandit.

Agua Dulce was a hiker friendly town. All the restaurants gave hiker discounts. I stopped at the Maria Bonita Mexican Restaurant and had the best enchilada rancheros I have had in my life. The grocery store knew exactly the foods hikers wanted and had them in abundance. There were so many tempting foods I spent nearly $90 and really felt the extra weight in my pack leaving town. Some grocery stores in towns along the Trail didn't have a clue what hikers wanted for resupply and probably didn't care. This grocery store made a tidy profit from hungry thru-hikers.

Heading out of town the Trail followed the road for three miles. I passed a house where a husband and wife and two teenaged daughters were unloading groceries from their car. The husband was watching me curiously as I walked by. Finally he asked: "Are you a thru-hiker?"

Yes.

"How far have you hiked?"

A little over four hundred miles.

"Wow! Power to ya."

Thanks.

"How many more miles do you have to go?"

Uh. Let's see. A little over two thousand-two hundred.

"Whoa! (Looking at his wife) He has **TWO THOUSAND TWO HUNDRED MILES left to hike!** Good luck, man. Power to ya."

"Thanks."

I was starting to feel a little depressed.

The next section had a reputation for being hot, mountainous, desert hiking. It was evening and as soon as I got off of the road I started looking for a place to put my tent. This was such rugged land that I hiked until dark and the only spot I could find was right next to a Trail register. I didn't know it but this was an area that hikers night hiked because of the heat. Once I was in my sleeping bag at least ten night hikers came by and signed the register. I never did see any of them but talked to them through my tent. It was kind of weird.

One of the night hikers was Listener. I passed her on an uphill grade the next day as she was slowly, methodically, making her way up the mountain. I said hello and continued on. She caught up to me an hour later as I was taking a lunch break next to a water cache. Listener was 74 years old. She was attempting to thru-hike the Pacific Crest Trail. She was an avid triathlete and eagerly told me about the events she had entered. She was about 5'3" and no more than 115 pounds. She had a pack that looked larger than mine. I loved her enthusiasm and determination. We chatted for quite a while. It was now June and this was an especially hot day with a lot of difficult hiking. You could not afford to miss any water sources. It looked like Listener only had three quart bottles for this section. This worried me. The next water source was a fire tank that had gotten bad reviews. I reached the fire tank far ahead of Listener. It was absolutely gross! When I pulled the lid off of the top, it smelled like a dead animal. I knew Listener would be running short of water so I waited in the shade of a nearby tree for over an hour. Finally Listener showed up with another younger hiker. He had given her extra water. I smiled. Hikers, particularly young hikers, looked after Listener. It was like they were looking out for their grandmother.

I made it to a lovely campsite in the pines that evening. I slept peacefully. Early the next morning I heard a muffled cough. I looked out of my tent and there was Listener cowboy camped under a giant oak not twenty feet away. By the time I had eaten some trail mix and gotten out of the tent, Listener was already hiking. That was one tough lady and I say that with respect. The last time I saw her was just before Lake Tahoe. I hiked with her for part of the day and camped with her that night. Her attitude was still great but it was painful to watch her wince as she slowly massaged her swollen fingers and knees. Her back ached so much she had to put her pack onto a rock and back into it. Every hiker knew of Listener. Even the last day on the Trail hikers were talking about her with a smile. I have a feeling when I finished she was still out there hiking.

The next day was spent trying to find water sources and trying to stay hydrated. I drank a lot of water. I ended the day at 6:00 pm, which was earlier than usual. If I hiked any further I would be heading downhill into an area that had been burned by a forest fire. I stopped at Horse Trail Camp. It was high on a ridge and overlooked the Mojave Desert. The views were superb. The Mojave Desert was vast. I would be traveling through it for the next three days. Just looking at it was intimidating. Miles in the distance was what looked like a square lake glistening in the sun. It turned out to be at least a mile square area of solar panels. I filled up my water bottles from an excellent spring. I had the campsite to myself until Scarecrow came in at 7:00 pm. He was in his middle twenties with a big beard. His clothes were not old and worn but they had big patches on them. His pants were baggy and came down a couple of inches below his knees. We tried to communicate but it was like we were from two different planets. There wasn't any animosity but after a while we both gave up and went to our tents. This was only the third time I had tented around someone else and that included the night before when Listener camped twenty feet from my tent. By eight-thirty I was in my tent with the flap closed and in my sleeping bag. Scarecrow was nearby in his tent quietly writing in his journal. It was starting to get dark and I was feeling drowsy enough to fall asleep A young couple came into camp:

"LET'S HAVE SOME DINNER, THEN WE CAN HIKE ON DOWN THE TRAIL AND FIND A PLACE TO CAMP."

"OK, SOUNDS GOOD."

"WHAT DO YOU WANT TO MAKE?"

"LET'S MAKE THE MACARONI AND CHEESE. DO YOU WANT TO ADD THE SALMON PACKET TO IT?"

"YEA."

They continued to loudly chatter as they made and ate their dinner. By now it was dark.

"IT'S GETTING LATE. DO YOU WANT TO SPEND THE NIGHT HERE?"

"MIGHT AS WELL"

Me: Shit!

"YOU CLEAN THE DISHES AND I'LL SET UP THE TENT."

"OK."

"BRAAAAAKKKK! MAN, THAT SALMON DIDN'T AGREE WITH ME. I DON'T FEEL TOO GOOD. BRAAAAAKKK!" (As he pounded his chest)

By now it was closing in on 9:30 pm and they didn't seem to be winding down. Finally they decided to get into their tent.

PPPPFFFFFTTTTTT "OH, GROSS!"

They lowered their voices to soft murmurs.

"STOP THAT!" Giggle Giggle

Me: Please, no.

They were still for a few minutes and I was thinking they were "finally" ready to go sleep. I started to relax and drift off.

"LET'S PLAN WHAT WE ARE GOING TO DO FOR TOMORROW."

"OK. LET"S GET AN EARLY START. HOW ABOUT 4:30?"

"SOUNDS GOOD. HOW FAR SHOULD WE GO? LET'S GET OUT THE MAPS."

Me: AAAAAAAAARRRRRRRGGGGGG!

I never deliberately camped around other people. By the time I found a campsite I was tired, and after eating, ready to go to sleep. I always tried to find a camping spot without any places nearby for other campers.

The couple really did leave at 4:30 the next morning and even tried to do it quietly. I slept in for another three hours. Scarecrow had extra water he had filtered and offered it to me before he left. That was thoughtful because the water source was down a very steep trail that, at times, I had to bushwhack to get to. We attempted some more small talk but it just wasn't happening so we said goodbye.

For the next eight miles I descended on a winding pathway through canyons to the desert floor. It was the 8th of June. The enormous, flat, Mojave looked like it was going to be hot and it was. I reached the desert floor at noon and in a couple of miles the Trail merged with the Los Angeles Aqueduct. It was about ten feet deep and twenty feet wide and made of concrete. The water was bright blue. I followed the Aqueduct for twelve of the twenty-seven miles I hiked that day. It was open for the first couple of miles then went through a wide pipe partially buried in the ground and eventually back to a flow way covered by thick concrete. The concrete was so thick there were car tracks on it. I spent hours walking on the Aqueduct listening to water flowing rapidly underneath. There used to be gaps in the Aqueduct where hikers could get water but they were closed after 9/11. Occasionally trucks patrolling the area would drive by and the drivers would wave. I didn't see another hiker the whole time I was walking along the Aqueduct. Many hikers walked through this area at night to escape the intense desert heat. It was hot but there was a slight breeze that felt good. The pathway was flat and smooth and I was hiking at four miles per hour. There were lots of cactus with bright yellow flowers, sage with its rich desert fragrance, apache plume covered with fluffy, red tinged plumes, and Joshua trees. I have always loved the colorful desert and felt right at home. I would occasionally pass an isolated house. They must have had an awesome view of the stars at night in the immense open space.

The Trail left the Aqueduct and I hiked three more miles before stopping for the night. I camped next to a brand new wind farm. It was so new the huge wind turbines weren't even allowed to turn yet. There was a water cache where I filled my water bottles and met Lezlie. It was only 6:00 pm but I was ready to call it a day. Lezlie was planning to hike until dark and cowboy camp under one of the desert trees. As we were chatting, a truck stopped next to the water cache. A man giving trail magic came down to visit. He had a couple of cokes and Snickers bars and was welcomed with open arms. If there is such a thing as a PCT thru-hiker groupie this man was it. He was really interested in our hike and asked a lot of good questions. He had been giving out trail magic for over ten years and met all the hiking legends. It was fun asking him about Billy Goat, a 74 year old hiker with over 40,000 miles under his belt, who hiked the PCT eight times and was hiking this year. I had to ask about my thru-hiking hero - Scott Williamson. Each year he hikes the PCT, often setting speed records. He was the first person to yoyo the PCT –hiking from Mexico to Canada and back in one calendar year. In twenty years he has hiked over 50,000 miles.

He was featured on "60 Minutes" a few years ago.

The man confirmed Scott Williamson is a genuinely nice guy who even on his speed record quests takes time to chat with awestruck hikers. I was hoping to meet him while I was hiking and I may have in Oregon but didn't realize it until later. I was heading north and passed a person heading south who was wearing a pack that looked smaller than most day packs. We were walking through a rocky area with loose footing and with long sure strides, he made it look effortless. We were wearing the same type of trail runners, even the same color, and as we passed he said: "Nice shoes." I said: "Thanks. Same to you." and we kept going. I camped with some other hikers that night and one of them asked: "Did you see Scott Williamson today? He was hiking southbound."

Before the Trail Angel left he asked Lezlie and I if he could take a video of us. He videotaped me first and started off by saying: "I'm interviewing a couple of the stragglers at the back of the pack. What is your trail name?"

I don't have a trail name yet so I'm going by my real name -Jim.

"Are you enjoying your hike?" I'm loving it.

"Do you think you will make it to Canada?" You Bet!

I hiked twenty-seven miles that day. I started a week and a half after the "Herd" and was already catching and passing a lot of hikers. I didn't think of myself as a straggler and it was kind of disconcerting to hear it but I let it ride.

He asked Lezlie the same questions and I learned her trail name was Shutterbug. He finished with: "Do you think you will make it to Canada?" Lezlie became visibly nervous. "Well.....I'm not sure.......I'm going to try.....that's a long way......"

So much of a successful thru-hike is mental. You have to have drive, focus, and the belief that you can do it and nothing is going to hold you back. I asked about Lezlie at various stages of my hike and never could keep track of her. Her love was photography. I'll bet she had a fun hike and took a lot of amazing pictures.

After the Trail Angel left, Lezlie and I talked for a while before she headed on. She reminded me a lot of my sister, Johanna. She was bright, interesting, and verbal. There were never any awkward pauses when we were trying to think of something to say.

This was wind farm country and the wind was doing its job. It was absolutely hellacious. There was a ten foot high by ten foot wide concrete wall positioned to block the wind. It was an ideal place to put a tent or cowboy camp. I decided to cowboy camp. I got into my sleeping bag and worked into a soft place in the dirt until I was comfortable. I closed my eyes and listened to the pounding wind. I was thankful for the barrier. Within a minute, two mice were vying for my attention. Great! I put up my tent with just the screening to keep the mice away and it worked. I didn't get much

sleep that night because the wind was too noisy and gusty, but it could have been a lot worse.

Most of the next morning was spent walking through the wind farm. The wind turbines were enormous. They were brand new and state of the art. The three blades were designed to swivel directly into the wind and were shaped like an airfoil to generate speed. I talked to another hiker who said that when this wind farm was on line it would generate more electricity than any wind farm in California. It was currently going through the certification process. They were losing a lot of money while they waited. I walked in the wind for hours. I had never experienced anything quite like it. There were no trees and nothing to block the wind. As I was trying to walk on the pathway the wind was pushing against me with such force I was pitched forward like a ski jumper flying off the ski ramp. Time and again gusts would push me off the pathway and I would have to work my way back. I'm sure I looked like a staggering drunk, weaving along the Trail. Finally I passed the last wind turbine and headed up into the mountains. Two miles into this strenuous hiking I met Lezlie at a water cache. The wind had taken it out of me and the cold water tasted delicious. I spent an hour with Lezlie before continuing on.

Lezlie was hiking the Trail in a unique way. He mother would try to meet her at the end of each day and they would drive to the nearest town and spend the night at a motel. They planned to do this all the way to Canada. Lezlie was going to meet her mother that evening at the road leading to Mojave, California. I was planning on spending the night in a camping area a mile before the road and hitching into Mojave the next morning. I took off ahead of Lezlie. It was mountainous, difficult hiking for the rest of the day. Four miles before the highway to Mojave I ran into another wind farm. The wind was even worse than in the morning. I was on a pathway near the top of the mountain and it took total concentration to keep from being blown off. I had on my wind shirt and was glad to have it. I had to take off my hat because the wind pushed the sides against my face and blocked my vision. A loose pack strap whipped against me and caught me on the cheek. It was turning cold. I needed my gloves but I needed to be able to grip my hiking stick without the gloves even more. I was jamming my hiking stick into the ground to keep from being blown off the side in heavy wind gusts. There were steep drop-offs and it was scary. A mile before the highway I passed the wind farm. I was hoping the wind would die down but it didn't. I looked at the campsite where I was planning to spend the night. It didn't look inviting. I was cold, windblown, and very tired. A night at a motel in Mojave was sounding good. When I reached the highway there was a parking lot next to the Trail. Lezlie's mother was waiting for her. I went over to her car and knocked on the window: "I hiked with your daughter this afternoon and she is about an hour behind me. Could I get a ride into Mojave?" She couldn't have been nicer. "Sure. Get into the car. You look like you are freezing. You're almost blue." She turned on the motor and turned on the heater. That felt soooo good. We talked for an hour before Lezlie showed up, just as cold, windblown, and bedraggled as I was. They could have been twins. They had the same hairstyles, mannerisms, speech patterns, and happy, positive outlook on life. Mary drove me to a Motel 6 and gave me a Subway sandwich and a Snapple Green Tea which she insisted I take. Lezlie gave me her cell phone number and told me to call when I was ready to head back to the Trail. The first thing I did after getting to my room was take a long, hot, shower. I had lost a lot of body heat and the hot shower felt great. It took a half an hour and two of the little bars of Motel 6 soap to get all the accumulated dirt off. It felt good to be squeaky clean. I finished the Subway sandwich in about five bites and went to bed. Motel 6 motels meet my needs exactly. They are clean, unpretentious, and the price is right. I decided to take a zero day to recharge and the cost for two nights, with senior discount, including tax, was $76.36.

Mojave was a small desert town of only about 4,000 people. The main road paralleled the railroad tracks. Trains came through all day and night. The Motel 6 was on the edge of town and within thirty yards of the tracks. There must have been a train signal that said - Hit Horn - because every train that came into town hit its LOUD horn at exactly the same spot! I was so tired I would be awakened by WWWWAAAANNNNNN as a train slowly came through town and would be asleep by the time the last freight car passed. I slept in as late as I wanted the next morning and lazily headed over to a nearby burger joint for breakfast. I got in line behind a burly construction worker. The lady taking the order was well past her prime but still trying: "What'll ya have, hon?"............."OK. That's a breakfast burrito and coffee. You get a discount for cash and I'll give you the "Handsome" discount." (Wink)

My hiker appetite was kicking in and I knew one breakfast wouldn't fill me so I ordered two of the biggest breakfasts on the menu. The price was amazingly inexpensive - even without the "handsome" discount. My stomach was actually growling I was so hungry. A waitress brought the two breakfasts to the table. She had a puzzled look on her face: "Where's your partner?" "It's just me." Her eyes grew wide and I could see why. The portions were absolutely huge. The three pancakes alone, which were just part of one of the breakfasts, were huge. I dug in with gusto! I have to sadly admit that for the first and only time, I was defeated. I left about a quarter of my breakfast burrito, which was literally dripping with grease, on my plate. Fortunately there were no other thru-hikers around to witness my shame. The rest of the day was spent resupplying, eating, lounging around watching TV, eating, and finally sleeping. I called Lezlie the next morning and they picked me up fifteen minutes later on their way back to the Trail. Mojave was an excellent rest stop.

The next twenty-five miles was a waterless stretch and I carried six quarts of water. At 2.2 pounds per quart that was 13.2 pounds of water. I was carrying ten pounds of food. My pack base weight was 14 pounds. I was carrying 37.2 pounds. Ugh!

My goal was to get to Kennedy Meadows and the start of the High Sierras within a week and out of the HOT desert. By this time I was tired of the oppressive, relentless heat. The next seven days were the hottest that I can remember. It was like the desert was saying: "I'm not finished with you yet, chump!"

Within the first mile I was hiking through another wind farm. Great! There were wind turbines for the next eight miles. There was a reason there were wind turbines for the next eight miles! The Freaking WIND!! I remember my excitement when I saw my first wind turbine. Believe me – that was long gone.

I was recharged after a rest day in Mojave and hiked twenty miles on one of the hottest, toughest days, period. The first eight miles before Interstate 58 at Tehachapi Pass were over brown, dry, dusty, rolling hills. Scraggly cattle grazed this area and it looked like their hoof prints covered every square inch while they scrounged for anything to eat. Lezlie's mother left me two quarts of water in a shady area next to I-58 and I drank one right on the spot. Thank you, Mary. It was an extremely hot day and the next ten miles were all uphill. I had my trail legs and even with the heavy pack, I moved rapidly uphill. Trains were working their way through the pass. Some of them had an impressive number of cars and five engines and it looked like all were in use. As I neared the top of Tehachapi Mountain the views out over the Mojave Desert were limitless. Far in the distance I could see the little town of Mojave with an enormous airfield next to it. One of the trains that passed me near Tehachapi Pass was almost to Mojave. It was so tiny I might have missed it if not for its motion. I made it to the top of the mountain in the evening and found a good spot to camp. I was tired but that much effort produced endorphins that created a very pleasant high.

----- Tehachapi High In California -----

Five miles into the morning's hike I stopped at Golden Oakes Spring. It was in a shady area under old oak trees. The water came out of a small pipe and was cold and pure. While I was eating some trail mix and enjoying the break, U-Haul joined me and five minutes later Jeremy showed up. At the end of the day I camped with Kieshi from Tokyo, Japan. It was odd to meet them all on the same day because these were three of the most determined hikers that I met on my thru-hike.

U-Haul was the first hiker who looked close to my age. He had just gotten back on the Trail after having to take care of some business back home. He had been off of the Trail for ten days and was trying to get back into shape. He was blistered and sore. He had grey hair and after talking with him for a while I realized he was probably closer to forty. We leap frogged all the way to Kennedy Meadows. He was disciplined and would be hiking each morning by 4:30. I tried to sell him on my idea of hiking from 7:30 am to 7:30 pm each day. It went over like a lead balloon. I should have taken a picture of that frosty look followed by: "You have to hike your own hike....I guess." He was a pretty fast hiker. That day I hiked 24 miles, then 25 miles, and 22 miles, and at the end of the third day he was ahead of me. I lost track of him after Kennedy Meadows and didn't see him again until forty miles past Crater Lake in Oregon.

It was astonishing to see the condition he was in. He had lost sixty pounds. There were dark rings around his hollow, haunted, eyes. They had an almost insane glitter as he talked to me. His mind and memory were very much intact. By Oregon I was used to seeing gaunt faces but his skin clung so tightly to his face it was startling. He had just taken eight days off because of illness and I didn't ask what it was. A lot of hikers were getting giardia and that would be my guess. He was hiking with Holstein and Tangent, a couple in their thirties. We took a break and caught up on other hikers we had hiked with. I got out my trail mix and they cooked some hot food. U-Haul looked at his food and looked nauseous. He could only eat a little. By Oregon hikers needed to be putting in enormous amounts of calories. He didn't have any body fat to burn. He looked like a disaster waiting to happen. I last saw him in Sisters, Oregon. He had a friend give me a ride back to the Trail which I appreciated. I kept expecting to hear of him getting off of the Trail but I would see his name in logbooks and registers in Oregon and Washington and he would always be two or three days ahead of me. Each time I would see his name I would say: "Hang in there, man! Hang in there!" He made it!

Jeremy was twenty-six and from New Zealand. He was easy going and courteous. He was typing a journal that was being read in New Zealand and apparently he had quite a following. He had been interviewed on New Zealand TV and the newspapers. I leapfrogged with him all the way to Kennedy Meadows. I enjoyed his company. Whenever he would take a break he would get out his computer with keyboard and start typing. He earned the Trail Name - Typo. He was extremely thin, almost frail looking. Most hikers were thin and wiry with a strong core. Jeremy didn't look like he had the core strength. I had the feeling if he made it to Canada he would have to take a lot of rest breaks and zeros. If he did make it, it would be because of sheer determination and character. After Kennedy Meadows I never saw him again. I did read his journal on the PCT-L web-site when I finished my hike. He made it to Canada two weeks after I finished. His last two days were, at times, in heavy snow and even whiteout conditions. I was delighted to see that he made it.

There was a lot of desert hiking that turned to forest by the end of the day. By 8:00 pm I made it to Robin Bird Spring. There was an excellent spring and camping area. Kieshi was in his tent and cooking dinner with his stove just outside the tent. I set my tent next to Kieshi, had some trail mix for dinner, and went to sleep.

About 10:00 pm I heard a faint - ping....ping....ping....ping.... I couldn't figure out what it was and went back to sleep. In the morning I packed up and headed out. Directly on the pathway between my campsite and the spring, Jeremy had put his tent. I had to squeeze my way between the tent and a fence to get by. When I saw Jeremy later in the day he was red-faced. He had gotten to the spring after dark, hadn't seen our campsite with his headlamp, and put down his tent thinking he was alone.

The next day was brutally hot. Kieshi started before me and I caught up to him by 10:00 am as he was taking a break. He was sixty years old although he looked forty. He could understand English and even catch the slang and humor but was painfully slow trying to express himself and very self-conscious. He liked the camaraderie of being with other people during breaks and tenting with them at the end of the day but he didn't talk a lot. He seemed like a nice, distinguished gentleman. Coming from Tokyo, with thirty million people living in a small area, it must have been a shock hiking in the vast open spaces of the PCT with nights full of stars and howling coyotes. Earlier in his hike he had suffered so much from the heat he was helped off of the Trail by other hikers and taken to the emergency room of the nearest hospital. As I passed him I knew the rest of the day was only going to get hotter. He looked miserable. He looked completely drained. I figured he would start searching for shade and spend the rest of the day out of the sun. He caught up to me later in the afternoon when I was taking a break. He still looked hot and miserable. I was surprised to see him. He had to be one of the steadiest hikers on the Trail. He couldn't hike fast but he did consistently put in a full day. He knew that with his lack of speed he could take very few zeros to make it to Canada before the snows. He left Kennedy Meadows the same day I did. I saw him again just as he was getting a hitch into South Lake Tahoe. That was the last time I saw him. He signed a register in Oregon and at that time was a week behind me. He had a quiet determination that I admired. I would bet money he made it to Canada, probably around the 13th of October, right when the rain and snow was scheduled to start.

He was the only thru-hiker in his sixties that I hiked with on the Pacific Crest Trail. I hiked with only one thru-hiker in his fifties. I met few hikers in their forties and not many in their thirties. The majority of hikers were between twenty and thirty. Many were around twenty-three, having recently graduated from college and hiking the PCT before entering the work force. I enjoyed and admired their youthful energy and gradually was accepted by many of them after leapfrogging with them for hundreds of miles. I enjoyed chatting with them during breaks, sometimes hiking with them for a couple of hours, or having a beer with them in town.

Day after day of scorching heat was beginning to wear on me. It was a harsh environment that made do with very little water. Areas that looked completely barren were actually teeming with life. There were big black lizards, horny toads, hummingbirds, vultures soaring high on thermals, loud squawking crows, black flies that loved to bite, and always - ants. There were many Joshua trees. They were spread out and formed little clusters for protection from the wind. They were only about fifteen feet tall. Usually they were too close together for a place to take a break. Once in a while there would be a small spot. Resting under the shady branches, it felt like an oasis from the baking sun.

That night I camped next to a Joshua tree. I was on the side of a small canyon. There was a light breeze that felt good because it was still warm. I found a place just big enough for my tent and pushed around the dirt with my shoes to level it. As I was staking down the tent I had to work around some prickly cactus that caught me a couple of times. It was dark by the time I finished dinner and got into my sleeping bag. It was a great location and I fell asleep immediately. In the middle of the night I was awakened by the howl of a coyote. It was a perfectly still night. There were no other sounds. Its high pitched, mournful, howl filled the air and echoed down the canyon. I lay in my sleeping bag, completely relaxed, listening to the beautiful, almost haunting, howls.

After a refreshing sleep I was ready to take on the next day. It was a good thing because this was probably the hottest, most barren area of my hike. I still had six quart water bottles and was glad to have them. I drank two and a half gallons of water that day. There was a water cache at Bird Spring Pass I would reach at noon and I had my fingers crossed it would have water. If it didn't I would have enough to reach the next source but I would be hurting. In the distance I saw Joshua trees where the water was cached. When I reached the cache it was completely full. There were tire prints that showed where a car had stopped, backed up, and turned around. They were still fresh. Yahoo! The Trail Angels of the desert really were!

There was water thirteen miles further at McIver's Spring. It was supposed to be absolutely gross. Hikers reported seeing toilet paper in it. Talking to other hikers the next day, every one of them had gotten water at McIver's Spring. Some of them even said it smelled bad when they filtered it.

Five miles into the next day's hike I was passing a campground and saw a sign: Trail Magic Next To The Blue Tent. I happily headed down. There was a large awning that covered an area for cooking and a picnic table. There were camp chairs in the shade.

Oakie Girl was the Trail Angel. As soon as she saw me she asked: "Would you like a breakfast burrito?" "Sure!" "Help yourself, there are sodas, coffee, even beer if you want it." The place was loaded with bagels, fixings for sandwiches, cookies, doughnuts, pastries, bananas, apples, oranges, chips. The breakfast burrito was excellent with sausage, hash browns, cheese, refried beans, scrambled eggs, and salsa. I demolished it.

Oakie Girl thru-hiked the Appalachian Trail and had hiked parts of the PCT. She knew about the hiker appetite and said the words all thru-hikers dream about: "Don't hold back, there is plenty of food. Eat as much as you want." And we did. U-Haul was already there. I came in next, followed by Jeremy, Kieshi, Shawn Murphy, Scalawag, and Bouncer. We put a serious dent in the food. So much so, Oakie Girl decided to make a trip to Lake Isabella to resupply. I was planning to hitch the twenty miles into Lake Isabella to resupply, so this was perfect timing.

I sat in the front seat and chatted with Oakie Girl as we drove to the grocery store. She spent about ten days each year giving trail magic and had been doing it for a number of years. She was retired and this was the way she was enjoying her retirement. She also had a Forest Service job part of the year. She was reliving her Trail experience through other hikers. She was good at getting a conversation going and participating in it without dominating it. She was thoroughly enjoying being a Trail Angel and her generosity was much appreciated..

By the time we returned most of the hikers had enjoyed a beer or two and were in a good mood. The conversation flowed freely. "Who wants hot dogs with chili?"

"Me! Here! Yea! Yo! You Bet! I Do!" Oakie Girl was becoming our hero. Hikers who wanted to have dinner, spend the night, and have breakfast the next morning were encouraged to do so. As we were eating hot dogs, Oakie Girl said she had seen a helicopter pass overhead the day before and hover over the nearby mountain. She heard a hiker had died the previous night. She didn't have all the details but heard it might have been caused by a bear. We all knew hikers who were a day or two ahead of us and were worried. After finishing my hot dog, I knew I needed to get going. There was a drumbeat in the back of my mind: "Bear! Bear! Bear! Bear!" Finally at 3:00 pm I reluctantly headed out. Oakie Girl gave me two apples to take along and I added a $5 donation to the tip jar. It's amazing what good trail magic can do for your energy and morale.

Within a mile I left the desert and it became mountainous and forested. There was a long climb along the side of the mountain and it was almost dark by the time I found a level spot to put my tent. I was camped on a saddle with beautiful views in both directions and an equally beautiful sunset to end the day. I ate my dinner well away from the tent and triple bagged my food. I would be lying if I said I slept like a log. I heard many sounds in the night. Some of them had my heart thumping. I was never happier to see the sun come up the next morning. I learned later the hiker who died was in his mid-fifties, was section hiking the PCT for a few days, and died in his sleep.

I started the morning hiking in a shady forest. After a couple of hours that changed and I hiked for miles through a burned area with absolutely nothing for shade. There were a lot of burned areas on my hike. I remember few of them. They were depressing and boring and I would grind and space out to get through them. Some of them took hours to get through. Occasionally there were areas that had a stark beauty. The trees had no bark and were so bleached by the sun they were a shiny white. Wind flowed through them creating a low moan.

I ended the day next to a gently flowing stream. Some thoughtful Trail Angels had left a tub full of beer in the water. With so much trail magic I was getting spoiled. I remember thinking: "What? No sodas?" It had been a long, hot, day hiking through way too much burned forest. I chugged the Tecate beer. I was feeling no pain as I happily and sloppily set up my tent.

The next day, I caught up with Typo, U-Haul, Scalawag, and a young couple that I didn't know. There were some big cottonwoods and everyone was taking a break in the shade. It was hot even in the shade. There was supposed to be a stream nearby but it was dry. For the last six miles we had been hiking down a narrow canyon in a forest fire area that was beginning to recover. It had been a dusty, sooty, hike. The last time any of us had taken a shower was at least a week earlier. Water was sparse and used mainly for hydration, not cleaning. I was filthy. I had intricate, white, salty, sweat stains all over my black shorts and red shirt. My legs were sooty, filthy, and had sweat streaks flowing down them. My arms were grimy and my face was smudged with soot. I looked at the other hikers. They looked worse than me! It gave me kind of a twisted satisfaction. That evening I found a level spot next to sandstone boulders to put my tent. I could see the High Sierras in the distance for the first time. I was only three miles from Kennedy Meadows.

2 THE SIERRAS

Kennedy Meadows and the start of the High Sierras had been a goal since the start of my hike. I was excited. I would reach Kennedy Meadows the morning of June 18th, spend the rest of the day resupplying and recharging, and head out the next morning. I was exactly on schedule. Kennedy Meadows was a tiny mountain town. There was a small store that had a big deck with lots of picnic tables, smaller tables, and snack bar. I had a bear canister, letter from Johanna, and resupply box waiting for me. The store owner took me to the back of the store to find my boxes. There were easily one hundred boxes lining the walls waiting to be picked up. I was impressed. "If you think this is a lot, you should have seen this area a couple of weeks ago." She had my boxes located in a matter of seconds and marked them off of her checklist.

All hikers entering the High Sierras had to have a bear canister. I carried mine four hundred and ninety-five miles from Kennedy Meadows to Sierra City and mailed it home. It sits on my kitchen counter and is my oatmeal container. It still has the postage sticker stamped from the Sierra City Post Office. If you were caught without a bear canister there was a hefty fine and the Forest Service did check. Forest Rangers stopped me twice to see my thru-hiker's permit and see if I had a bear canister. The canisters weighed almost three pounds, were made of tough, clear plastic so you could see the food inside, and were bear resistant.

I watched a video where a huge grizzly was tossing the canister around trying to open it. I was focused less on the canister than the size of that bear. I regret seeing that video. Hikers grumbled about carrying the extra weight but bear canisters were helping the Forest Service get control of the bear problem. I grumbled with the rest of them but it was a pleasure to have everything with a bear attracting smell, in the canister and fifty feet from my tent.

When I packed my resupply box at home to send to Kennedy Meadows, I estimated needing two pounds of food a day. I figured it would take six days to get to Independence, which was my resupply point in the Sierras. I sent seven, two pound packages of food to Kennedy Meadows, giving myself a small cushion. By the time I received my resupply box at Kennedy Meadows I knew I was only eating a pound of food a day. That gave me fourteen days before having to resupply. I changed my plans. Instead of stopping in Independence I decided to try to make it 175 miles to Vermillion Valley Resort in twelve days. That was only14.5 miles a day average and would give me a two day cushion of food. It didn't sound that difficult and I made it, but boy was I wrong! With the bear canister and fourteen days of food, my pack was HEAVY – 45 pounds. It was harder to pick up my feet, particularly at the end of the day, and I started to stumble over rocks more than normal. The bear canister made the pack taller and it had a tendency to sway. I had to concentrate to keep my balance. I slipped and fell a couple of times and with the extra weight I hit hard. The Sierras went up in altitude to over 13,000 feet. I was hiking a lot in the 11,000 plus range. It took a while to adjust to the altitude. There was a lot of climbing. With the altitude and extra weight, I had to stop often on climbs to catch my breath.

The area I was traveling through was absolutely gorgeous! I decided to hike the High Sierras just like I had hiked the 100 Mile Wilderness in Maine. Slow down and thoroughly enjoy it. It was an excellent decision.

Right from the start I knew the High Sierras were something special – something truly: "Once in a Lifetime". As I was hiking through them I was thinking in superlatives – spectacular, magnificent, awesome, incredible, mesmerizing, gorgeous! I would walk into an area that was so awesome I would say to myself: "It can't get any better than this." An hour later it would be even better. I could stop, turn in a complete circle, and the views in every direction were stupendous! This happened over and over. Day after day. If a Shan-gri-la exists, it would have to be the High Sierras. It was like traveling back in time to an area that hadn't changed in 10,000 years.

From the time I started climbing into the mountains until I reached Red's Meadow Resort 200 miles later, I never saw a road. The only travel was by foot or horseback. I was always surrounded by towering mountains - enclosed in my own little world. The only reminder of civilization was the occasional plane passing overhead. So many things were out of scale. Granite walls would be so sheer and massive that it was intimidating. Standing next to them I would be looking straight up. The forests were old growth with no evidence of forest fires. Many of the surrounding mountains were full of glaciers that created waterfalls. The sound of cascading water echoed off of canyon walls. Water was everywhere and glacier cold, sparkling, and pure. I would kneel down by a stream, fill my water bottle, and drink to my heart's content. The glaciers created high mountain lakes with deep, blue water. Sunlight sparkled on the water creating millions of little diamonds. It was mesmerizing. Some areas were nothing but rocks and glistening lakes for miles. Other areas were forested and green. The abundance of water created dark, rich soils, lush green grasses, and an abundance of bright, colorful, flowers. Little lakes were right next to the pathway with water so clear I could see all the way to the bottom.

I was fortunate to spend much of the time in the High Sierras alone. There weren't any human sounds. I was listening to the trickling flow of a stream, the crashing sound of a waterfall, the splash of a fish catching a fly and falling back into the water, water gently lapping onto the side of a lake, the scree of a hawk soaring high overhead, the call of a marmot, or the high pitched whistle of a pica.

The beauty of the High Sierras is far beyond my powers of description. This was one time when I wished for a good camera. Quite a few times the thought struck me that Doug would have gone nuts in this area. The sheer beauty would have kept him clicking his camera almost non-stop. It would have taken him weeks, months, even years, to get through the High Sierras. "Has anyone seen Doug?" "Last I saw him was back in '15. He had a big beard, hair down to his shoulders, and was focusing his camera on an old, gnarled, bristlecone pine. Legend has it he's still out there."

It took days to hike over the many passes in the High Sierras. Forrester Pass was the first and highest at 13,200 feet. It was steep and switch backed and I stopped about every two hundred yards to catch my breath. As I neared the top, I couldn't figure out which was the actual pass. There were four options and none of them looked good. A couple of them looked terrifying. Finally the pathway narrowed, it became steeper, and the switchbacks tightened. The drop-offs were steep and the footing was rocky and slippery. I stayed as far away from the edge as I could. I hugged the side if truth be told. This was tricky without snow. I couldn't imagine doing it in snow and ice. I finally made it to the top. I felt a mixture of relief and exhilaration. Other hikers made it to the top and there were bellows of triumph and many pictures taken.

The descent was steep with a lot of switchbacks. The pathway was rocky. There were small loose rocks and rocks as big as softballs. I descended slowly, relying heavily on my hiking stick to stay upright. The views were so gorgeous it was hard to concentrate. I was surrounded by towering, glacier covered, granite mountains. There were sparkling lakes far below. Adrenaline was flowing through my body and I felt wired and great. I hiked over Glen Pass, Mather Pass, Selden Pass, and Muir Pass. At Muir

Pass a stone hut had been built in the 1930's to honor John Muir. I walked inside. There was a big stone fireplace, seating built into the wall, and a tiny window with sturdy glass. It was dark and musty inside. Voices echoed. It had a feel of history to it.

I was joined at the top of Muir Pass by Cactus and Extra Credit, a couple in their early twenties, Mister Wizard and Dubbs, also a couple in their twenties, and Trip, a New Zealander in his mid-twenties. I hiked with and around them all the way to Red's Meadow Resort. They were a fun group to be with. They had a positive energy. If ever I had wanted to hike with a group this would have been the one. They invited me to hike with them. Cactus even tried to give me a trail name. He and Extra Credit caught up to me as we were hiking in the early morning. Cactus acted excited like he had something special to tell me.

"Jim, I've been thinking on it, and I have a trail name for you."

Really? (Gulp!)

"Yea. POO BEAR!"

Poo Bear? (WTF?)

"You know. Poo Bear. Like in "Winnie the Poo". Your voice is kind of high and you have an easy going disposition. POO BEAR! That's your new trail name! What do you think?"

Poo Bear. Well, it sounds interesting.

He could see I wasn't entirely delighted with it and Extra Credit looked skeptical, too.

"You can turn down a trail name if you don't want it but I think it's a good trail name - Poo Bear."

Let me think about it, Cactus.

When we caught up to Mister Wizard, Dubbs, and Trip, Cactus was all enthusiasm.

"Jim has a new trail name. It's Poo Bear!"

No one was sharing his enthusiasm.

"Poo Bear?"

"Yea. Like in "Winnie the Poo".

Dubbs (Who was cute herself): "It sounds kind of cute."

Extra Credit (Still skeptical): "You don't have to take it if you don't want to......"

Mister Wizard (With his baritone voice): "I ain't calling him Poo Bear."

Trip: "Me either."

The newly anointed Poo Bear: Let's try it out for a while and see if it works. A big smile crossed Cactus' face. I kept the trail name Poo Bear for the next few days as I was hiking with the group. Dubbs and Extra Credit were very attractive women. I liked it when they called me Poo Bear with their feminine voices: "Hi, Poo Bear."

They all started calling me Poo Bear after a while and I was tempted to keep it but eventually they took a long break at Mammoth Lakes and I never saw them again. I was pretty sure I would stay ahead of them so I went back to Jim.

As I was heading downhill later in the day I came across a level, sandy spot perfect for putting my tent. I was in an area surrounded by glacier covered mountains that formed an amphitheater. There were waterfalls nearby and the sound of the falling water echoed in the canyon. There were many streams heading down from the glaciers. The streams converged and became Evolution Creek. Evolution Creek ran through a wide, grass filled valley. I knew I would be crossing Evolution Creek the next day and it was creating anxiety. In heavy snow years, river, stream, and creek crossings could be very difficult, even dangerous.

Yogi's Handbook told where the dangerous crossings were and gave hikers' accounts of what it was like when they attempted to cross. Some of the accounts were pretty vivid. Evolution Creek was one of them. I reached Evolution Creek early the next morning. It was a lovely setting. I stepped in. The clear, clean, water was iced cold. I walked across easily in water no deeper than my knees. When I crossed Bear Creek later in the day the same thing happened. The water wasn't even up to my knees. Hikers in years past had described it as one of the most dangerous crossings on the Trail.

Getting closer to Vermillion Valley Resort I had finally eaten most of the fourteen pounds of food. The hiking was still difficult but I could feel the difference in the way my pack balanced and being able to lift my feet. The rocks along the Trail were as bad as the rocks of Pennsylvania and my feet were starting to go numb at the end of each day. This had me worried. I was hoping they wouldn't get worse because I was having a great time and didn't want to have to end my hike. Other hikers were having the same problem and it gave me some comfort to know I was not alone. I had given myself a two day food cushion from Kennedy Meadows to Vermillion Valley Resort. Although I only averaged 14.5 miles a day from Kennedy Meadows to Vermillion Valley Resort, the energy expenditure was enormous. I only had a handful of food left.

There was a six mile long lake between the Trail and the resort. Most hikers were picked up in the morning by a boat and returned to the Trail in the afternoon. I was ravenous and had eaten nothing but trail mix for the last twelve days. Instead of paying $18 dollars for the round trip boat ride I decided to hike along the lake and spend the money that I saved, on breakfast. I was up early and hiking by 5:45 am. I was motivated. I had food on my mind. The six mile hike along the lake was fun. There was even a small, sandy, beach where I took out my cleaning cloth, dipped it into the water, and tried to make myself half way presentable. This resort depended on thru-hikers to make a profit. It was a hiker friendly place geared to making it easy for hikers to spend money. There was a sign just before the entrance that said: "Hikers - Please Loiter". It was good for a chuckle. By the time I left I realized the owner really meant it. I entered the little restaurant. There were two couples having breakfast. They looked at me like a novelty but soon went back to their conversations.

I ordered the breakfast burrito. It was expensive but it was massive and good. Just as I was finishing the burrito the couple seated at the table next to mine got up and left. The man had ordered pancakes and had eaten less than one quarter of the three huge, fluffy, golden brown, pancakes. They looked delicious. I couldn't take my eyes off of them. I was dying to stick my fork into those puppies and swing them onto my plate. I came so close to asking the waitress if I could, but I chickened out. I did settle for chocolate pie a la mode. Delicious!

The resort had a small area with food for a resupply. There wasn't much to choose from. Previous hikers had pretty much cleaned the shelves. There was a Wasabi Trail Mix and I picked up a couple but almost everything else was junk food. When I went to the counter to pay, the cashier rang me up and asked if I wanted to put it on a tab. I had been asked the same thing at the restaurant. She had a memorized list of things to ask me which included the price:

Do you want to take a shower? We have towels you can rent. No.

Do you need to do laundry? No.

Do you want to take the boat back to the Trail? No.

The bar is open in the afternoon and we have a thru-hiker special. You can put the drinks on your tab. No.

She was clearly getting frustrated. Each time I said no, there was a little sigh. I spent twenty-five dollars for the breakfast including the tip and fifty-three dollars for overpriced junk food and I was being made to feel guilty for not doing my share?

I headed back to the Trail. I followed the little path beside the lake. After four cups of good coffee and an excellent breakfast, I felt happy and well fed. This was still the Sierras and the hiking continued to be magnificent. There was a big climb to start and the hiking stayed difficult for the rest of the day. I had energy to spare. By the afternoon I had climbed into the 11,000 foot range. I was out of the forest and into a high valley. I passed mountain lakes and winding streams with tiny waterfalls. Areas next to streams were covered with red, yellow, and purple flowers. The air smelled of fertile earth and peppermint. In rocky areas I passed marmots next to their dens. Sometimes they would let me get within a few feet of them.

At the end of a hard day of hiking I found one of the most perfect camping spots of all. I was high in the mountains in a wide valley about a quarter of a mile from Silver Pass Lake. I could see Silver Pass in the distance. I would be climbing it the next day and it looked daunting. A stream heading from Silver Pass Lake was nearby. I could hear its gently splashing water. I found a soft, sandy, spot to put my tent. There were no human sounds, just solitude, and wide open spaces. I intentionally got out of my tent in the night. The full moon was bright. I could see everything so clearly. My body was casting a moon shadow as I gazed at a sky absolutely covered with stars.

Hiking to Silver Pass was tiring. I noticed I was taking more breaks on climbs and the numbness in my feet continued to worry me. Later in the day I entered a thick forest. I started running into trees that had fallen across the Trail. Sometimes there were impromptu pathways around the trees. Other times, I could climb over the fallen trees and not detour from the pathway. Some of the fallen trees were thick and hard to climb over. A lot of the time there were branches I could grab onto and pull myself up and lower myself over. I was always banging my legs doing this. Throughout my hike there were scabs on my legs that were in various stages of healing and new wounds where the blood had trickled down and was starting to dry. All of a sudden I entered an area where big, healthy trees had toppled. They were all over the place. Some trees had fallen on top of other trees. These were a challenge to get over. It was slippery, and awkward, and the higher I climbed the more dangerous it became.

From Vermillion Valley Resort to Red's Meadow Resort, I passed hundreds of downed trees that crossed the Trail. Trail maintenance crews had done an absolutely incredible job of cutting these big trees and opening the pathway. When I passed these crews, hard at work, I literally tipped my hat to them and thanked them.

A freak wind storm in the winter had caused devastation in this area. When I was talking with Sprinkles way back at Cajon Pass, he told me about the wind storm. Apparently the wind from this storm came from the opposite direction. I can't remember the exact wind directions Sprinkles told me about, but I think that over the years, trees had adapted to wind coming from the west. The root systems were much denser on the west side to better anchor the trees. When the huge winds came from the east, the root systems weren't strong enough and the trees were blown over. Tens of thousands of trees were blown down. It was sad to see perfectly healthy trees, some with thick trunks and quite old, lying on the ground. I hiked over forty miles through this devastation.

A few miles before reaching Red's Meadow Resort, I hiked through an area that had been ravaged by fire and wind. Many of the burned trees had been toppled by the high winds. Some had been snapped in two about ten feet above the ground. I tried to imagine the power of a wind storm that could do that. The Trail was full of ash and soot and looked lifeless. Not quite… A badger was hiking the PCT, too. It came around a corner and headed right toward me. It was fifty feet away, making little grunting sounds and moving like a little low to the ground tank. It hadn't noticed me. Now it was twenty feet away. I tapped the ground with my hiking stick. It looked up, jumped straight into the air, did a 180 degree turn in the air and took off down the Trail in the opposite direction.

The Trail passed close to Red's Meadow Resort. It had a small cafe that was supposed to have excellent milkshakes and I was looking forward to stopping there. There were streams along the Trail where I could have cleaned up a bit, but after a while, trying to stay clean each day lost its importance. If you had seen my grubby hands, stained with dirt, you would have been appalled. When I stopped for breaks and ate my trail mix, I didn't clean my hands. It's hard to explain. I knew when I needed to clean my hands and I did, but it was rarely more than the once a day that was mandatory. I never once was sick on my hike. Mosquitoes became a problem for the first time in the Sierras. I used a mosquito repellent called Ultrathon. It was designed for soldiers in the field and was very effective. It lasted a lot longer than the Deet I used on the Appalachian Trail. There was one problem with it. Once I put it on, if it came in contact with dust or dirt, it became dark and made my face, arms, and particularly my legs, look filthy. Did I want to look like a model for GQ or keep the mosquitoes away? I became the poster boy for "Hiker Trash".

Hiker Trash was a term Pacific Crest Trail thru-hikers used with pride. When you hiked ten to twelve hours a day it was easy to get really funky. You were sweating all day and that collected on your clothes. After a while, they reeked. Sweat, mixed with the dirt that accumulated on your body, created a body odor that had people opening windows if you were hitchhiking, or moving away from you if you were standing next to them. You had permanent bedhead. Your fingernails were caked with dirt. Your hands had to be seen to be believed. Your feet were absolutely filthy. If you took off your shoes, the smell was noxious. Your legs and arms were covered with dirt and soot if you hiked through forest fire areas. Your face was smudged with grime. When you were with other thru-hikers you didn't notice the smell. I always worried when I saw thru-hikers who were overly fastidious. If they obsessed about keeping their hands clean, or their clothes clean, that was not a good sign. If I saw them again two hundred miles down the Trail and they were as grubby as me, I breathed a sigh of relief.

Once, as I was walking to town, I headed toward a woman on the same side of the road. When she got within twenty yards, she crossed the street. I smiled and waved and she looked straight ahead. When I looked in the mirror later in the day, I actually was scary looking. One thru-hiker was offered a pair of socks by a lady who thought she was homeless. Another hiker was taking his clothes to the laundry in a plastic bag and was stopped by a man who said that he could add a few cans to his collection. As uncle John would say: "I think you get the picture." Thru-hikers who made it past the half-way point were hard and lean. They stunk. Their clothes were worn, ripped in places, stained, and faded by the sun. They had deep tans, thick calluses on their feet and hands, scabs on their arms, legs, and hands, and bug bites everywhere. You could look at another hiker and tell if he or she was a thru-hiker. Far from being embarrassed by the way we looked and smelled, it was a source of pride. When you were called "Hiker Trash" by another thru-hiker it was a compliment.

Finally, I made it to Red's Meadow and the tiny cafe. There was a counter and seven tables. I was the only person at the counter. Three girls between eighteen and twenty sat down at the table behind me. This was a tourist area and they were definitely tourists. They had seen some other thru-hikers outside and were talking about them in low voices. They could see I was a thru-hiker and were keeping their voices low thinking I couldn't hear what they were saying. I could. It wasn't flattering. Soon, I was joined at the counter by Dubbs and Mister Wizard. Dubbs was having foot problems and their group was heading to Mammoth Lakes to stay as long as it took for her feet to get better. Trip came in and headed toward us.

Picture Jim Bridger, Jeremiah Johnson, Jedediah Smith, and Trip heading toward you. He looked like a Mountain Man. He looked wild and untamed. He was 6'2" and 220 pounds of solid muscle. He took off his hat and his bright red hair shot out in all directions. He had a full, dark red, untrimmed beard. His face was smudged with dirt. His clothes were dirty and worn. One of the girls said under her breath: "Look at that onnne." I glanced back expecting to see disapproval. Not even hardly! Their eyes were sparkling!

After an excellent double cheeseburger and chocolate shake, I headed back to the Trail. I left Red's Meadow on the 3rd of July and reached Tuolumne Meadows on July 5th. Because of its beauty this was a popular area for hikers. The Trail was loaded with people enjoying the 4th of July holiday. They were out to have a good time and their cheerful enthusiasm was infectious. Red's Meadow was a resort and horse packing station. I had seen few horses on my thru-hike. Just outside of Red's Meadow I was passed by a grizzled old cowboy leading twenty fully packed horses. There was a younger cowboy in the rear with a bandana over his nose who was eating a lot of dust. The old cowboy stopped and chatted for a couple of minutes. With his weathered face, he looked like he had been doing this all his life. A couple of hours later a family on horseback approached me high on the side of a mountain. There was a steep drop-off to the river below. On the other side of the river the mountain rose steeply and there were canyons, glaciers, and waterfalls. We stopped and talked for a while. Sharing the Pacific Crest Trail with horseback riders was an enjoyable part of the thru-hike experience for me. Our mode of transportation was different but we both shared a love of the outdoors.

Along the sides of mountains were small streams that crossed the Trail. Usually I could hop over them. Often they were full of thick vegetation. After the parched desert, I was still enjoying the abundance of water. I would stop frequently to drink the iced cold mountain water. There were big, green meadows full of birds. Such a variety of beautiful bird calls. Sometimes I would take an impromptu break, find a spot to sit down, and enjoy my own little symphony of bird calls. I passed Thousand Island Lake. I had seen pictures of a gorgeous high mountain lake on the wall at the Red's Meadow café. This was it. I walked beside the Tuolumne River for the last eleven miles before reaching Tuolumne Meadows. I passed people fishing and families having picnics. I made it to the huge campground by 2:00 pm. There was a large area just for backpackers. I paid $5, picked a spot with a picnic table and bear box, and put up my tent. This was one of the biggest campgrounds I had ever been in. It looked to be completely full. It was fun wandering around and checking things out. Having gotten used to the solitude of the forest, my senses were bombarded with the squeals of children playing, barking dogs, loud music, people partying, and the wonderful aroma of meat being barbequed over a fire.

There was an area where people gathered in the evening to listen to talks by Forest Rangers. A Ranger was nearby talking to a couple of people. She was talking about bears. We had been warned you could almost expect a bear to wander through the Tuolumne Meadows Campground in the night, so I listened in. The Forest Service was really getting the bear problem under control. From mile 753 entering Sequoia and Kings Canyon National Park until leaving Yosemite National Park at mile 998, hikers were required to use bear canisters. If you were caught without a bear canister there could be a hefty fine. There were nineteen bear boxes (food lockers) next to camping areas between mile 760 and 949. These boxes were made of thick metal and effective.

The Forest Service would re-locate a bear if it lost its fear of humans and started going after food. If the re-located bear went back to its old habits, it was killed. From Yogi's PCT handbook, I knew where the problem bear areas were from Campo, California to Manning Park, Canada. I circled the bear areas on Halfmile's maps. I never camped in one of those areas during my hike and never had a problem with bears. I heard the Forest Ranger say there hadn't been one bear encounter in the campground in 2012. Good job, Forest Service. Keep up the good work.

I continued on my walk. The campground was so convoluted that I got lost. It took a while to find my way back to my campsite. Big PCT thru-hiker. It was embarrassing. I had a hard time sleeping in the campground that night. There were so many noises I wasn't used to and too many people that were too close.

The next morning I headed over to the little store that was geared toward tourists. It was 9:00 am and already there were buses unloading tourists. The place was packed. I needed to resupply and was surprised at how well stocked the store was for thru-hikers. It was expensive but there was an excellent variety of trail mixes and bagels, and unfortunately, what was becoming one of my favorite foods - Nutella. Almost all hikers raved about Nutella. After looking at the ingredients, the first being sugar, I held off buying it for a long time. It had a chocolate taste and spread over a bagel, was a real treat. Maybe it was psychological, but any time I used Nutella, it gave me an immediate boost of energy. By the end of my hike I was eating the stuff by the spoonful. There were picnic tables in front of the store and I brought my food supplies over to one of them, tore off all the packaging, and organized them to put into my bear canister. I still had one of the packages of Wasabi trail mix left. The wasabi peas had been hard on my teeth. When I crunched down on them to break them, a little voice in the back of my mind kept telling me to throw them away. I came so close to doing it but my instincts said I would be throwing away calories and I needed calories. I was joined by some curious tourists. Almost every time I talked with tourists or day hikers I would be asked at least one of these questions:

1. Do you carry a gun? Hell no.
2. Have you seen any bears? Yes.
3. Have you seen any mountain lions? No.

They had extra chocolate chip cookies which they gave me before they left. I devoured them on the spot after giving them a heartfelt - thanks.

I had enough food to make it the 75 miles to Sonora Pass. It was a sunny day with clear blue skies. Within the first mile I reached Soda Springs. It had markers that told about its history. One marker was next to an old wooden shed that surrounded a soda spring. There was a picture taken in the 1860's of men next to the shed, with their tin cups, drinking the water from the spring. I dipped my water bottle into the same spring and took a drink. Yeech! It was heavily carbonated. I don't know if it was a sense of history or what, but I kept sipping from that 32 ounce bottle for the next two hours before I finished it, going - Yeech! - each time I took a sip. When I would unscrew the top of the bottle it would make a loud – fzzzzz.

One of the markers said this was where John Muir formulated his ideas for the development of our National Parks. The area around Soda Springs is breathtakingly beautiful. He would bring writers, poets, (including Emerson), congressmen, and others, and show them the beauty of Nature and the need to preserve it. John Muir was born in 1838 - 175 years ago. He is still the man who is talked about and quoted the most by thru-hikers.

As a nation we are indebted to John Muir. He is one of my heroes. Many times on my 2,660 mile thru-hike I marveled at what a beautiful country this is. Often I was looking over vast areas that were forest or desert as far as I could see. Think of all the life being lived in those areas; the animals and insects and plants and grasses and flowers and trees. John Muir, through his writing and actions, influenced people to preserve that natural beauty. He talked about the giant sequoias that were thousands of years old. They were being logged at the time. There is a picture of loggers next to a sequoia they had just cut down. They were dwarfed by the circumference of the tree and were smiling proudly for the camera. That picture truly made me sick. That tree had been growing for over two thousand years. The sheer arrogance of businessmen who looked at it as nothing more than profit!

Imagine how much our forests would have been exploited if not for John Muir, or even if we would now have National Forests. I compare him to Abraham Lincoln. Lincoln is rightfully considered one of the best, if not the best President ever. What would have happened if we had had a weak, indecisive leader? Would we even still be the United States of America?

John Muir came along at a time when we needed a pragmatic, inspiring, visionary. Through his leadership we have National Forests that are the envy of other nations and enjoyed by millions of people each year. He even co- founded the Sierra Club to help conserve our forests. He served as its president for twenty-two years. The Sierra Club now has over 1.3 million members. Here are two of my favorite John Muir quotes:

"Climb the mountains and get their good tidings. Nature's peace will flow into you as sunshine flows into trees. The winds will blow their freshness into you, and the storms their energy, while cares will drop off like autumn leaves."

"Man must be made conscious of his origin as a child of Nature. Brought into right relationship with the Wilderness he would see that he was not a separate entity endowed with a divine right to subdue his fellow creatures and destroy the common heritage, but rather an integral part of a harmonious whole."

So the least I could do was drink that nasty carbonated water from Soda Springs. Here's to you, John.

Hiking for the next five days until I reached Sonora Pass was some of the most beautiful, varied, and rugged of the whole hike. My body was taking a pounding on the steep, rocky terrain. There were blow downs everywhere which added to the workload, and lots of river and stream crossings. It was fun hiking. It was true wilderness. There were swiftly flowing streams and twenty foot waterfalls that formed pools deep enough to swim in. I wasn't about to, but a lot of hikers did, and I would hear their cries of alarm as they plunged into the iced cold water. Time and again, I would cross a stream or river where Halfmile's maps or Yogi's Guidebook warned of a difficult or potentially dangerous crossing. Most of the time, it was little more than ankle deep.

Sometimes after stream crossings it would be difficult to pick up the Trail. I would have to go upstream and downstream looking for it. Once, I crossed in an area where two streams converged and found what I thought was the Trail and continued hiking. I noticed the footprints I had been following were no longer there. There were secondary prints that looked kind of familiar, so I didn't stop, get out my map, and make sure I was on the Trail.

Most of the time on the Pacific Crest Trail it was easy to follow the shoe or boot prints of the hikers ahead of you. In many areas thru-hikers were the only people on the Trail. After a while you knew who was ahead of you by their prints. The most popular shoe on the Trail was the Brooks Cascadia 7 trail runner. I bought four pair of them before my hike and had them mailed to me about every 650 miles. My normal shoe size is a 7. Having been warned that my feet would expand with all the wear and tear of a thru-hike, I purchased size 9's. It worked out perfectly. It was a comfortable, light, and durable shoe. Only once did one of my shoes rip and it was minor and only thirty miles before reaching Canada. I noticed that thru-hikers developed an efficient hiking style. There were never any pigeon-toed footprints or duck walks. When I hiked near towns with a lot of traffic on the Trail, the pigeon toes and duck walks would show up.

I had been following the footprints of Manparty and Lush. I remember thinking:

"Manparty and Lush took the wrong turn. They are going to be pissed when they realize it." I continued hiking for another three miles as the Trail became less defined. I kept selling myself that I was still on the right Trail: "I know those secondary prints belong to Dave. He should be about a half day ahead of me."

Finally I stopped, got out my map and GPS, and figured out my location. It took less than a minute to realize my mistake and how to correct it. I tried to put a good face on it - "lesson learned" - but I've got to admit, I was pissed having to backtrack three miles.

This day was spent hiking up and down mountains, fording streams, climbing over blow downs, showing my bear canister and thru-hiker permit to a Forest Ranger, and finishing the day high on a mountain next to a stream that provided a constant, soothing sound that lulled me into a deep sleep.

Part of the next morning was spent hiking on top of a mountain. The long distance views were gorgeous. Benson Lake was circled on my map as a must-see area. Dr. Pflueger, who takes care of Fred, and has taken care of Wingo, and even Nipper when he was a pup, stopped there when he was on a horse-packing trip and highly recommended it. I reached the turn-off to Benson Lake and headed down. The trail had not been maintained and was overgrown with grass. There were blow downs everywhere. There were swarms of mosquitoes. After a hundred yards, I turned back.

The Pacific Crest Trail was also full of blow downs in this area. Some were piled on top of one another. It was challenging getting through. I even lost the Trail for a few minutes. I was disappointed not being able to get to Benson Lake, but at least I could tell Dr. Pflueger I was able to see that big, beautiful lake in the distance as I hiked by.

This was a hard day of hiking. I hiked twelve hours and could only account for eighteen Trail miles. The six mile detour didn't help.

The next day was challenging but enjoyable. I ended at Wilma Lake just as it was getting dark. As I was putting up my tent, I was absolutely swarmed by mosquitoes. There were hundreds of them. I didn't have any Ultrathon lotion on and they were covering my body and biting. I have never experienced anything quite like it. I would brush them off and in two seconds they would be back. I immediately put my head net on and about twice the recommended amount of lotion. It worked. The mosquitoes were still swarming around my body but weren't landing. I hurriedly set up the tent, hopped in, zipped up the netting, and cursed the ravenous little buggers.

When I woke the next morning, I could hear a constant drone — nnnnnnnnnnnnnnnnn. They were waiting for me. I put on my head net and loaded my body with Ultrathon lotion. I wore the head net almost all day and appreciated not having to be constantly waving my hands in front of my face as I walked by stagnant ponds and marshy areas. I crossed a river where I actually got my feet wet and found a spot under big, shady trees to take a lunch break. I was just finishing the Wasabi trail mix when I crunched on one of the wasabi peas and felt my tooth break. It was the tooth furthest back on the bottom right side of my mouth. I spit out the food and saw pieces of tooth and filling. I felt the area with my tongue and could feel a big gap and the jagged edges of what was left of the tooth. I knew I still had to eat, so I took all the peas out of the trail mix and took a bite. There wasn't any pain from the tooth but its jagged edges cut into my tongue, which started bleeding. I had to position the food in my mouth so the edges of my broken tooth had the least contact with my tongue. The only food I had left was the trail mix which had lots of nuts, granola, and dried fruits. It was difficult to chew and painful. I was two and a half days from Sonora Pass and a hitch into Bridgeport, California to find a dentist. I had to gingerly eat food each day, trying to keep my swollen tongue from bleeding too much. The hiking in this area was difficult. It was rocky and slippery. I was putting in big miles and needing even more calories than normal. My broken tooth wouldn't allow me to put in the number of calories I needed. My body started feeding on what little fat I had left, to make up the difference. I could feel a drain on my energy, particularly later in the day. It was a miserable two and a half days. One thing helped. The area I was hiking in if anything was more gorgeous than ever.

The next day I reached the 1,000 mile mark. I had been on the Trail exactly two months. Right at the 1,000 mile mark there was a solid piece of metal about eight inches wide, fifteen feet long, and eight feet above a swiftly flowing stream. I anxiously made my way across, wondering how many people over the years had made it all the way to the 1,000 mile mark and fallen into the stream. A fall while wearing a backpack would have caused serious injury. Pocahantis and Chef were there to congratulate me. Earlier, they shot by me on a steep, rocky, downhill with Pocahantis in the lead. There were drop-offs on some of the turns and they were going dangerously fast. I think they were a couple. Pocahantis looked to be in her early twenties and very pretty. Chef looked like he was nearing forty and as he passed me, staying right behind Pocahantis, I could hear him groaning on the bone jarring descent.

Later, I was passed by Trooper who was hiking with Pocahantis and Chef and trying to catch up to them. Whoever gave him his trail name got it right. He was a big man with a thick, bushy, mustache. Put sun glasses and a trooper hat on him and he would be the guy telling you: "Driver's License and Registration, Please." The man oozed testosterone. He shot by me four times that day. He would come barreling towards me and when he was right behind me would bark: "PASSING ON YOUR LEFT!" I would jump three feet in the air, clutching my heart! As he passed he would say in the same voice: "THANK YOU, SPORT!"

The next day was one of the most beautiful that I can remember. I spent much of it above tree line hiking along volcanic ridges with fantastic views of mountains and valleys in all directions. It was a wide open area. I could see the Trail miles in the distance as it wandered down past glaciers, small mountain lakes, and glacial streams before heading up through meadows full of colorful, mountain flowers. From high on a ridge I could see Sonora Pass. There were cars in the parking lot and I wanted to get there right away to see if I could get a hitch into Bridgeport. As the crow flies it looked to be about a mile. The Trail had other plans. Meander would be the perfect word to describe the next five miles. Instead of heading down to the pass the Trail swung to the right and paralleled the side of the mountain, drifting past small ponds and snow patches and through thickly wooded areas. It meandered in the direction that would find the most beautiful route down the mountain. My impatience gave way to appreciation and respect for the designers of this section of Trail. It couldn't have been more beautiful. When I daydream about the Pacific Crest Trail, the gorgeous volcanic ridge hiking and meandering descent to Sonora Pass always comes to mind.

I made it to Sonora Pass by 6:00 pm. It was about a thirty mile hitch on Highway 108, at Sonora Pass, to Highway 395 that went to Bridgeport. I didn't relish the thought of hitch hiking in the dark on Highway 395. I decided if I didn't get a ride within fifteen minutes, I would camp at the pass.

A sport utility vehicle came up to the pass from the opposite direction. It stopped and a thru-hiker hopped out. I waved at the driver and the hiker. After the hiker left, the driver came over. "I can give you a ride to 395, are you interested?" "Sure." There was a Marine base close to Highway 395 and he was a civilian mountaineering instructor. He had been a soldier in Afghanistan. He trained soldiers to go into the mountains of Afghanistan to engage the Taliban. As we drove down to Highway 395 he told me about training the Marines. I learned about pack weight, leadership development, and the teamwork necessary to carry out a mission. It was interesting.

I told him about my tooth and after mulling it over for one second, he decided to drive me all the way to Bridgeport. I couldn't have been more grateful. When he dropped me off he gave me a Spaghetti and Meatball Parmegian MRE (Meals Ready to Eat) which he said was one of his favorites. Round trip, he went forty miles out of his way to help me.

I asked a nearby policeman if there was a dentist in Bridgeport. There wasn't. He said the nearest dentist was about thirty miles away. Things were not looking good. It was close to 7:00 pm. I decided to get a motel room and try to figure out what I was going to do. If I did hitch hike to the nearest dentist, would he be able to see me right away? Would I have to wait a day or two or more? I learned that most dentists no longer do extractions; that you now go to an oral surgeon. The words "Oral Surgeon" set off alarm bells with dollar signs included. So I get to the dentist and he sends me to an oral surgeon, probably in South Lake Tahoe. That means more hitch hiking. Will the oral surgeon take me in right away? I was getting a headache.

My aunt Nancy Pryor, her son, John, and his wife, Sharon, live in Clovis, California about ninety miles away. I mulled over giving them a call and asking for their help. That was asking a lot of them. I really didn't want to make that call. I went back and forth in my mind before calling Nancy. I explained my situation and ended by saying I would certainly understand if they weren't able to do it. Nancy was nothing but gracious. She needed to talk with John and Sharon and said she would get back to me in an hour. Nancy called back right when she said she would. She said John would pick me up at 1:00 pm the next day, that he was looking forward to the drive in the mountains, and that Sharon was going to call her dentist and try to schedule an appointment for me. Mega sigh of relief.

John showed up at 1:00 pm the next day. We had lunch and headed back to Clovis. I stayed with the Pryor's for the next four days. They went out of their way to make me feel at home. I saw the dentist on the second day and he ground my tooth down, smoothed it, and put a hard cover on it.

I was greatly relieved that I didn't have to deal with a pulled tooth, which was what I was expecting.

When I arrived at the Pryor's I was tired. I had been pushing hard since I entered the High Sierras over three hundred miles earlier. I had pushed extra hard the last three days to get to Sonora Pass, had not been able to put in enough food, and had not slept well. There was a slight numbness in my feet and my heart rate, even in the morning, was elevated. I looked anorexic. My shoulders were all bones and my ribs stuck out. I needed rest and lots of food to recharge my depleted body. I got both in abundance. It felt great to sleep on a soft, comfortable, bed and sleep as long as I wanted. The Pryor's plied me with great food in abundance. They were Trail Angels Extraordinaire! By the time they drove me back to the Trail I was thoroughly rested, recharged, and ready to go.

The year before, in 2011, I attempted to thru-hike the Pacific Crest Trail and lasted four days. My mind wasn't in it. I flew back home. A family was staying at my house and expected to stay there for five months. I headed to the San Pedro Mountains in New Mexico in my trailer and camped and hiked for a month until a big forest fire closed the forest. I decided to head back to the Pacific Crest Trail and try a long section hike from Sonora Pass to the Canadian border.

On July 15, 2011 Nancy, John, Sharon, and their son, Aaron dropped me off at Sonora Pass. On the drive to the pass I noticed a lot of snow on the mountains and I was apprehensive. Starting at Sonora Pass, I hiked four miles before I had to turn back. It took me six hours to do that. By the time I finished I was a bloody mess. My legs were bloodied from breaking through the snow. I had gotten too close to a stream and broken through the ice. I hit hard in the water and instead of my right leg bending at the knee the normal way, it had bent in the opposite direction causing immediate pain. My elbows were bloodied and I left a big red patch on the snow. The Trail was under snow and I realized how miserable I was at reading maps. I saw what I thought was the Trail, high on the mountain, and maneuvered toward it. I crossed little streams with painfully cold water. There were lots of gullies and sometimes I would work my way up the side, lose traction, and slide back down. I finally made it to the Trail. It lasted about one hundred yards before it was covered again in snow. I followed footprints in the snow. There were steep drop offs to a swiftly flowing stream one hundred feet below. The Trail became impassable. I decided to find an alternate route. I didn't have an ice axe or micro-spikes, just my rubber soled trail runners. I made big Z's in the snow down the side of the mountain and finally made it to the stream. I was lucky to find a narrow area along the stream and plunged across. The iced cold water was over my waist.

I could see where the Trail should go along the side of the mountain and followed an imaginary line with my eyes until I saw the actual Trail in a break in the snow. I headed toward it. I followed a tiny stream part way up. It was steep and snowy and turned icy. I continued climbing with one foot in the snow and one foot in the icy stream. The ice won and I slid down on my front about ten feet. My clothes were covered in mud. I decided to tack up and finally made it back to the Trail. The Trail had areas that were in shade where the snow was easily five feet high. I post holed through those areas with my feet going down into snow above my knees and sometimes to the bottom of my shorts. I hit an icy patch and slipped off of the Trail. Fortunately there wasn't a steep drop-off and I only slid down about five feet.

When I made it to the top, for some reason that is beyond me, I still wasn't ready to throw in the towel. The Trail alternated between snow and a dirt footpath. I came around a corner to an area that was almost always in the shade. A thirty foot, icy snow patch covered the Trail. It was angled slightly downhill. There were footprints where hikers had dug into the ice to make their way across. Right next to the pathway was a sheer 500 foot drop. If I slipped and fell I would have tumbled 500 feet over jagged rock. There was no way I could have stopped my fall. To this day I don't know why I didn't turn back. I get chills thinking about it. Once I made the decision to continue, I totally focused on the footprints in the ice ahead of me. I took each step slowly, positioning my weight and hiking poles for best balance. I didn't allow myself to look over the edge. It took about ten minutes to go the thirty feet but I made it. When I reached the other side and shook out the tension, my hands were shaking. I continued on. Within two hundred yards I came to another ice patch that was even longer. I remember thinking: "This is crazy!" I turned around. Now I had to re-negotiate that thirty foot ice patch. I was really dreading it! I felt lucky to have made it across and I knew that now I was really pushing my luck. I looked at the drop-off. Shit! I didn't have any options left. With a great deal of trepidation but a lot of focus, I headed back over the ice. After I made it across, my whole body started shaking. Not uncontrollably, just vibrating. What awful judgment!

I finally made it down the mountain and stopped a mile before Sonora Pass. I found one of the most beautiful places I have ever camped. There were 360 degree views of tall, snow-capped mountains. The moon was making the mountains shine. I could hear a stream softly flowing in the distance. I stood quietly, thankful to be alive.

The next morning I headed to Sonora Pass. I decided to hitch hike to South Lake Tahoe and catch the Trail at Echo Lake to continue heading north. It was snowy and icy hiking north from Echo Lake. In some areas I was hiking over eight feet of snow and could hear the water flowing rapidly underneath. After two days I knew I couldn't safely go any farther. I hitch hiked north to Sierra City and spent a day trying to hike north, but it was too dangerous. I hitched north again to Chester and hiked for two days until I hit a raging stream. I searched upstream and downstream to find a place where I could safely cross. I realized it was too dangerous and ended my hike.

I use 2011 to show the difference a year can make. Back to 2012, exactly one year later. When I headed north from Sonora Pass there was no snow on the ground. The Trail was dry. The major streams were still there but the dozens of minor streams were gone. The area was alive with wildflowers. In a macabre way, it was fun re-visiting the places where I had the most difficulty. From high on the mountain I could see where I had broken through the ice next to the stream and strained my knee. It took months for the pain to go away. The tiny ice filled stream, which I tried to climb and slid down ten feet in the mud, was gone. Approaching the shaded area that had been snow and ice packed, I felt a tinge of apprehension. It was completely dry. I looked at the drop-off right next to the Trail. It was even steeper and more dangerous than I remembered. I shook my head in disbelief. What awful, awful, judgment! I continued on. I noticed if I had not turned around when I did the previous year, I would have hiked in snow and ice for another mile. The Trail stayed high on the mountain. The views were gorgeous so that's where I camped for the night.

The High Sierra's had lowered my daily mileage and after taking four days off, I knew I would really have to pick up the pace. In my tent that night, with my headlamp shining on my calendar and my trusty little pen in hand, I calculated how many miles a day I would have to average to get to the Canadian border by September 22nd. September 22nd was the day I completed the Appalachian Trail, so it provided a goal to shoot for and hopefully it would give me a safety factor to get to Canada before the snows. Some years the snows hit in early October and made the high mountains in Washington impassable. The distance from my present location to the Canadian border was 1,607 miles. The number of days until September 22nd was 69. 1,607 divided by 69 = 23.3. I had a regular sized calendar with one inch square blocks for each day. At the end of each day I would fill in the daily miles, total miles hiked from Campo, and the highlights of the day. When I divided 1,607 by 69 on the calendar, without a calculator, my calculations showed I would need to average 22 miles a day to get to Canada by September 22nd. Actually 22 miles a day turned out to be the ideal number for me. I couldn't have averaged 23 miles a day. Twenty-two miles per day pushed me to the limit but I could do it. All the way into Oregon I thought the 22 miles a day average would get me to Canada by the 22nd of September. It actually would get me to Canada by October 1st. I followed the plan of averaging twenty-two miles a day religiously for nine hundred miles. It worked beautifully. By nine hundred miles, I had formed the habits and discipline I needed to maintain that average without becoming a slave to it. Maintaining that average from Sonora Pass in California to far into Washington, kept me even with many of the young thru-hikers. They would pass me over and over and we got to know one another and developed a mutual respect. By late Washington, youth prevailed. I couldn't keep up the twenty-two miles a day pace and the young hikers passed me by. I missed them.

My next resupply was going to be Echo Lake which was 77 miles from Sonora Pass. It felt good to be hiking again. The first day was strenuous. I could feel the layoff. The second day was more challenging with lots of climbs and descents and views of deep valleys. By the third day I noticed something I hadn't felt in a long time. All the food and rest at the Pryor's was paying dividends. For the first time since the start of the Sierra's, the little layer of fatigue was gone. The numbness in my feet was gone, too. I had a spring in my step. It felt good to be able to push hard on steep climbs, knowing I was going to rapidly recover. I hiked twenty-four miles the fourth day, catching up to Listener in the afternoon. What a pleasant surprise. I hadn't seen her since the hot desert, 800 miles earlier. We spent some time catching up as we hiked along a wide, green valley. We found a place to camp five miles before Echo Lake and spent a chilly evening beside a crackling campfire as we chatted before going to bed.

I needed to pick up a resupply box at the tiny Echo Lake Post Office. It had limited hours, so I wanted to get there early. I left before Listener and reached the Post Office by the time it opened. The Post Office was part of a small store that supplied the residents who lived along the shore of Upper and Lower Echo Lake. The only way they could get to their vacation homes was by boat. This was expensive property and the people standing in line to purchase food were well off. They hadn't seen one another for at least a year and were catching up. It was interesting listening to them trying to top each other on achievements and travels. It was like listening to dueling annual Christmas letters.

The store had a deli and I ordered two ham sandwiches, a chocolate shake, chocolate chip muffin, and two extra-large chocolate chip cookies. There was a picnic table in front of the store and I sat down to eat my food and open my resupply box. That's where I met Nate and Jenna. Of all the people I hiked with, they were my favorites. They had both recently graduated from college and were hiking the PCT before entering the workforce. They were enthusiastic and positive and having a great time. I hiked with them or around them for the next twelve days. At times they motivated me to hike bigger miles than I was used to hiking. They were genuinely nice people. Both had a good sense of humor. They were bright, articulate, interested, and interesting. Like me, they spent many nights tenting alone and loved it. They took fewer rest breaks than I did but always tried to find a location with a knock out view before they took one. Sometimes the view would be so good I would stop and take a break with them.

Starting at Echo Lake, I hiked twenty-five miles through the Desolation Wilderness. It was a popular area that was well cared for and beautiful. All hikers had to have a permit to enter. I hiked along Lower and Upper Echo Lake. There were fancy speedboats shooting through the water. People were swimming in water that looked iced cold. Others were sunbathing on their decks. I felt like a voyeur looking down on them from thirty feet away. Nate and Jenna caught up to me and we got to know one another as we hiked. A young couple out for a day hike stopped them: "You're Nate and Jenna, aren't you? We've been reading your journal on PCT-L. We really enjoy it!" They chatted with their fans for a few minutes and headed on. They were thrilled to know people were reading their journal. After another mile I stopped for a break and let them continue on.

I passed Lake Aloha where I camped the year before. The whole area at that time was covered in snow. I had camped on a big, flat, rock, right next to the water. The water was almost completely covered with ice and snow and there were big icebergs sticking out. A wind blew over the water in the night and I froze my butt off. A marmot peeped into my tent early the next morning to see if everything was ok. This time there was no snow or ice anywhere.

Clouds were low and passing overhead rapidly. I hiked around lakes, next to waterfalls and swiftly flowing streams. There were canyons with sheer walls and colorful wildflowers everywhere. The Desolation Wilderness had it all. In the afternoon I started a climb to Dick's Pass. I was trying to find a place to put my tent but couldn't find any spots that had been previously used, so I continued on. The clouds continued to move rapidly overhead. There was no tree cover. As I made a steady climb up the mountain I started to get battered by the wind I knew had to be there. As I was nearing the top I was working hard not to be blown off of the Trail. When I reached Dick's Pass the wind was absolutely howling. Dick's Pass had a level area and in normal circumstances would have been a great place to camp, but I couldn't have put up my tent if I had wanted to. I started to descend. The sun was down and it was getting dark and cold. I added all my layers of warm clothes and was still chilly. At least I was in the trees which helped block the wind a little. I descended all the way to Dicks Lake before finding a place to put my tent. I was twenty feet from the water. There was still a strong wind and I had a hard time getting the tent up. The wind was coming off of the water and I put the tent behind a five foot high, ten foot wide boulder. All night long the wind howled. I would hear gigantic gusts crossing the water before they crashed into my tent. It was loud and next to impossible to sleep. I felt the lack of sleep the next morning. The scenery kept my interest but I was dragging.

I made it through the Desolation Wilderness by noon. The beautifully maintained Trail immediately became overgrown. I was on the side of a mountain with a small lake one hundred yards in the distance. I pushed through waist high shrubbery so thick I couldn't see the ground in front of me. My right foot hit a rock and I started to stumble. I took three fast steps, almost caught my balance, but the weight of the pack pushed me forward and I fell HARD on a big rock. My right arm, halfway between the elbow and the wrist, took the brunt of the fall. It completely tore off a flap of skin the size of a silver dollar and was bleeding heavily. I headed down to the lake to clean my arm. I took out my cleaning cloth, Neosporin, and a big bandage. The wound was full of dirt from the fall. Fortunately my cleaning cloth hadn't been used since the last time it had been in a washing machine. The water was full of pollen from nearby reeds and I cleared that aside. I soaked the wash cloth and gently cleaned the wound. I had to rinse and clean it a number of times until it looked good enough to cover with Neosporin. I put on a big bandage that completely covered the wound. I have a good immune system and heal fast. The bandage kept the wound well covered, so my strategy was to leave it alone and let it heal by itself. I figured in three weeks when I took the bandage off it would be completely healed. I finished the day on top of a mountain under tall pines. I could see white sailboats in the blue waters of Lake Tahoe.

Most of the next day was spent ridge walking. I stopped on a ridge near the turnoff to the Tahoe Rim Trail. There were commanding views in all directions. One view had Lake Tahoe in the background. There was a small meadow next to the pathway with yellow and red flowers and pine trees. I decided it was too good of a photo opportunity to pass up so I waited for hikers to come by. Five minutes later a couple about my age showed up. They were section hiking and had thru-hiked the PCT four years earlier. They were dying to tell me about it. As we were talking, a couple of more section hikers showed up. They were super enthusiastic. It was a perfect day and this was an ideal place to sit, relax, enjoy the views, and have a good conversation. The views all day were fantastic. From the mountaintop I looked down on Squaw Valley, home of the 1960 Winter Olympics. I camped on a ridge high in the mountains. I was starting to make an extra effort to camp on mountaintops. On calm nights they were excellent places to camp. It stayed light longer and the views and sunsets could be spectacular. That night, on the ridge, I found a spot in a meadow just big enough to put a tent. Surrounded by fragrant purple flowers it felt snug and cozy. There was a gentle breeze and I fell asleep immediately.

The next morning, Jenna and Nate caught up to me four miles before Donner Pass. They were faster hikers and would slow down to have a conversation. Sometimes they would hike with me for miles when we found interesting things to talk about. Nate's family met them when they reached Echo Lake and they had taken two days off. They were well fed by his parents and Jenna was telling me about all the wonderful food they had eaten. I had been eating uninspiring trail mix for the past few days and her description of the food was making me hungry. After a particularly savory description, I growled: "O.K.! O.K.! That's Enough!" She looked back thinking she had offended me and there was an immediate twinkle in her eyes. "But wait…….. I haven't told you about the dessert." She proceeded to go into exquisite detail. My mouth was watering. I began to moan. Nate looked back a little concerned, and I could see him get it. He smiled. "I had a beef burrito with pinto beans, melted cheese, lettuce, and green chili that was so huge it filled the plate. The best burrito I had in my life. I barely finished it, and then for dessert….." I moaned loudly: "You're killing me back here……" They laughed.

From day one, there was an unspoken competition between us. In the afternoon, there was a long hike up the side of a high mountain with lots of switchbacks. The Trail was visible for over a mile. Looking back, I could see Nate and Jenna a quarter of a mile in the distance. I was determined not to let them catch me. I started hiking as fast as I could. They could see me and I think it motivated them to put in a little extra effort. Each time I looked back they were closer. There was half a mile left to the crest and I was hiking with a drive and determination that almost bordered on anger: C'mon! C'mon! C'mon! C'mon! With a hundred yards to the crest, I looked back. They were less than a hundred feet behind me. Sweat was soaking my shirt and my breathing was ragged but there was no way I was going to let them catch me! I made it! Man that felt good! I wanted to do a little Rocky dance. I was so pumped I just kept going full out. I walked for a long time on the crest of the mountain enjoying the views. I would occasionally look back and I was actually pulling ahead of them. I ended the day on top of a mountain in the middle of a two hundred yard long, thirty yard wide saddle. I was loving this mountaintop camping. It was a calm night. I leisurely set up my tent, had some trail mix, and got ready for bed. As I was enjoying the sunset I noticed some non-threatening clouds far on the horizon. I went to bed by 9:00 pm.

About 11:00 pm I heard some distant thunder. Lightning flashes would light up my tent. I couldn't tell which direction the storm was heading. It was way in the distance so I went back to sleep. I woke up an hour later. The wind had picked up and there was now about a ten second difference between the lightning and thunder. The storm was moving fast. The intervals were down to five seconds and it was getting loud! My tent was the highest object on the saddle. I needed to get out of the tent, down to lower ground, and into the trees. I quickly put on my long sleeved shirt, my wind shirt, and yellow rain jacket. I took a garbage bag to cover my legs, put on my headlamp, hat, and shoes, and headed for the trees. It started to pour. I reached the trees, headed downhill for another one hundred feet, and found a level spot under a clump of small trees. I sat next to a tree and curled up with my hands around my knees. The garbage bag covered my legs and the hood of my rain jacket covered my hat. That's the way I stayed for the next three hours. At times a storm would be right overhead. A bolt of lightning would hit nearby lighting up the black sky. I would curl up tighter waiting for the immediate thunder which was amplified by the mountains. A lot of people die from lightning each year and this was on my mind. The intensely bright flashes of lightning and incredibly loud thunder scared the hell out of me.

By 3:00 am the brunt of the storm had passed and I headed back to the tent. I was wet and cold. The headlamp batteries were low and I could only see twenty feet ahead. I found the Trail but my tent was twenty yards from the Trail and the light from my headlamp wasn't powerful enough to illuminate it. I sloshed around, shivering in the drizzling rain for fifteen minutes before finally spotting the tent. It felt good to put on warm clothes and get into my sleeping bag. I was still wired but also tired and eventually sleep won out.

At 6:00 am I heard another storm approaching. In New Mexico I would watch a storm develop and see it slowly heading my way giving me plenty of time to prepare. Now I knew how fast storms developed in the California mountains.

I quickly got out of my sleeping bag and started stuffing things into my backpack. The storm was approaching at breakneck speed. Lightning and thunder was flashing and crackling. I threw everything out of the tent, got out, and started rapidly taking down the tent. I was the highest object on the mountain.

CCCCCRRRRRRAAAAAAKKK BBBBOOOOOOMMMMMMM

"That was too close! Should I make a run for it and leave everything behind? No. I've just got a little more to go. C'mon! C'mon! C'mon!"

Nate and Jenna passed on the Trail. Jenna was bouncing up and down and hollering at the top of her lungs: "HURRY!, JIM.......HURRY!"

CCCCCCRRRRRRAAAAAKKKKKK
BBBBBBBOOOOOOOMMMMMMM

"OH MAN! OH MAN! OH MAN!   C'MON! C'MON! C'MON!"

I pulled out the tent stakes, folded them into the tent, jammed it into the backpack and sprinted for the trees. Hail was pelting me and I hardly noticed. Talk about an adrenaline rush! Once I was off the top of the mountain and in the relative safety of the trees, I hunkered down and waited out the storm.

Right in the middle of this total chaos, as I was frantically trying to get my tent down, knowing I was the highest object on the mountain, wondering if the next bolt of lightning was going to kill me, and Jenna yelling: "HURRY!, JIM......HURRY!", I was thinking: "Forest Gump!" Jenna's voice sounds exactly like Jenny's when she yelled: "RUN! FO-REST......RUN!" as Forest was being chased by a bunch of bullies in a pickup truck."

The rest of the day was spent dodging thunderstorms. At one time, I was on the side of a mountain with no cover and could see a storm heading my way. There were trees far in the distance. It was a question of whether I could get to the trees before the storm arrived. Each clap of thunder increased my speed along the ground. By the time I reached the trees, I was flying! I was lucky to make it. That storm had hail the size of marbles. I was sheltered under a tree and still had a few pieces of hail painfully bounce off of my body.

There were two days near Big Bear with rain and snow. That was the only other moisture in over 1,700 miles of hiking in California. Most days were cloudless. After a while I wouldn't even look up to check the weather when I got out of my tent in the morning. It didn't rain once in Oregon. I had been warned that much of the hike through Washington was going to be spent in rain. It was described as cold and constant, sometimes mixed with snow. It rained the first two days in Washington and I was thinking: "Here goes...." It never rained again.

On the Appalachian Trail I was usually hiking under the canopy of trees. I hiked during thunderstorms. On the Pacific Crest Trail I spent hours in treeless areas, totally exposed to the elements. It would have been extremely dangerous to hike during a thunderstorm in those conditions. It would have been a pain in the butt having to wait out thunderstorms. I was fortunate to have hiked the Pacific Crest Trail in 2012.

3 NORTHERN CALIFORNIA

That night, I camped five miles before Sierra City, California. My plan was to get there by 9:00 the next morning, resupply, and head out by 11:00 am. As I was taking down my tent in the morning, Magic Bag stopped to chat. He was outgoing and talkative and I knew right away he was going to be a friend. There was a kindness about him, a good sense of humor, and an obvious enthusiasm for the thru-hike that made him fun to be around. I don't know how he did it but he hiked in sandals and was fast. He started his thru-hike a week after I did. He was in his early twenties, short, and built like a fireplug. I would see a lot of him all the way to Etna, California.

I made it to Sierra City by my 9:00 am goal. It was a cool little mountain town (population 200) and was one of my favorite trail towns. It was a hiker friendly town. Hikers really did have an impact on their economy and the residents knew it.

Sierra City was a gold mining town in the 1860's when it had a population of 3,000 people. The main street was still lined with some of the buildings dating back to that period. The Sierra City Country Store was in one of those old buildings. It is owned by Larry and Kathy Breed. Larry is in his sixties. He took over the store from his father and it might go further back in the family than that. There is a picture of Larry and his family taken in front of the store when he was ten years old. He and his wife were consummate professionals - polite, friendly, helpful. They knew what hikers needed for resupply and had it in abundance. They had every pop tart flavor available and the favorite of thru-hikers (Cinnamon) triple stacked. They had all the flavors of Ben and Jerry's ice cream. There was a deli in the store with items like the Triple Gut Buster Burger that had to be seen to be believed. It was a thru-hiker favorite. Hikers had their picture taken trying to chomp down on the Gut Buster.

I'm a burrito fan and they had a beef and bean burrito that was out of this world. I followed that with a pint of Ben and Jerry's Chocolate Chip Cookie Dough ice cream, a twelve ounce cup of coffee with extra cream and sugar, and I was good to go.

I had been told before reaching Sierra City that I had to check out the Red Moose Inn. Often I am skeptical if a place gets a lot of hype. Too many times in the past they were complete disappointments. With a full belly and happy smile on my face I headed over. Bill and Margaret Price took over the Red Moose Inn in 2010 and were terrific. It was in a big old house. There was a bar next to the dining area and a big outside patio with plenty of tables and chairs under shady trees. There were two rooms for overnight guests. It was totally geared for hikers and the only people at the Inn while I was there were hikers. Breakfast was served early in the morning. There was no lunch. Dinner was steak or ribs which Bill barbequed on a grill on the patio. When the tables inside weren't being used for dining they were being used by hikers. There was a computer, free phone service, an impressive hiker box, free showers with towel, free washer and dryer with loaner clothes, free camping in the back yard, and free coffee.

The bar was full of hikers and I even had a local beer to at least do a little toward generating some income for these generous people. I met hikers I hadn't seen since the early desert. As I was talking with Nate and Jenna, they mentioned they were going to try to average twenty-five miles a day to get to Chester, California. Chester was 138 miles away. I wished them the best of luck and told them how much I enjoyed hiking with them.

Maybe it was the beer – I don't know. I started mulling it over in my mind: "Can I average twenty-five miles a day or should I stick with the safe twenty-two miles a day average that has gotten me this far uninjured?" I felt like I was in the best physical condition of my hike so far, so I decided to go for it. It turned out to be a decision that had unexpected consequences for Jenna, Nate, and myself.

Drinking my beer at the bar I was in a relaxed, congenial atmosphere. Instead of leaving at 11:00 am as I planned, I left closer to 3:00 pm. It was the 24th of July. Heat was radiating from the pavement on the two mile road walk back to the Trail and sweat was dripping from my nose and chin. Nate and Jenna caught up just as we reached the Trail. We hiked together for the next half hour. The next four hours were all uphill. It was rocky most of the way. As I gained more than two thousand feet in elevation I watched the little town of Sierra City got smaller and smaller. It was a challenging climb but I was well fortified from the burrito, ice cream, coffee, and beer, and I had energy to spare. Nate and Jenna never did catch up.

That night I didn't sleep well. I was restless and heard too many sounds. There was a picture at the Red Moose Inn that was taken in the1860's. It was on the main street of Sierra City. I could see the Sierra City Country Store, the hotel across the street, and other buildings that are still around today. There was a donkey in the middle of the dirt road. It was on its side with a terrified expression on its face. On top of it, completely straddling it was a huge bear. The donkey was dying a horrible death. There were about fifty people standing in doorways and along the sidewalks watching. None of them was trying to stop it. That picture just brought me into it. I felt pity for the donkey. I was in awe of the ferocity of the bear. I felt disgust for the people enjoying this sad event. Meatheads!

The next day I hiked 27.5 miles. I was hiking with Nate and Jenna in the afternoon, and Nate, who was leading, came to a good sized blow down. He was 6'2" and athletic and made it look easy as he climbed over. Growing up, Jenna was a competitive gymnast. She still had the body and posture of a gymnast. It was like she was on a trampoline. Boing – Boing - and she was over. I tackled the tree attempting to - Boing - over. Fortunately, Nate and Jenna kept going so they didn't see my struggles. The – Boing - didn't happen. It took me about three minutes to get over. No justice! I wallowed in self-pity for a while but soon got over it.

The next day was difficult hiking. There was a two hour descent to the Feather River. Near the bridge was a deep, wide, pool. Hikers were splashing in the water. It was a hot day and the water looked cold and inviting but I passed. There was a hard four hour climb up the other side. I hiked 24.5 miles and was happy with that. I found a beautiful spot - almost - on top of the mountain to camp.

There was a lot of crest hiking the next day. The views were memorable. I caught up to Nate and Jenna at 7:00 in the evening. I had been trying for the previous hour to find a spot to camp without any luck. They found an ideal spot on top of the mountain. There was a tiny space right next to their tent that they offered me. I would have been three feet from them and it felt like an intrusion. There was a five mile switch backed descent to the Belden Resort. I told them I would keep going for another half mile and try to find a camping spot and if I didn't, I would head back. Nothing showed up in the next half mile. By that time the thought of hiking steeply back uphill after having already hiked 25.5 miles was not appealing. I still had 4.5 miles to find a camping spot. Surely something would show up. Nothing even close to a level spot showed up.

I ended the day next to railroad tracks beside the Feather River. I mean Right next to railroad tracks! I was thirty feet away at the most. I found a spot that had been used a lot. It was already dark. This place didn't feel right. I had the feeling it was illegal to be camped there. I looked for a No Trespassing sign but couldn't find one. I put my tent beside a fire pit. There

were empty cans that were scorched on the bottom. It looked like a hobo camp. There was a small road ten feet from where I camped. Once I was in my tent a car drove slowly by and I willed it to keep moving. Trains came by in the night. I could feel the vibrations of their powerful engines before they reached me. When they slowed, their wheels squealed loudly on the tracks. Once in a while they would let off steam – SSSSSSSSSSSSSSSS. They hit their horn before reaching Belden. A train horn from thirty feet at 2:00 in the morning is memorable! I gladly left at first light.

The Belden Resort was less than a mile away. Its restaurant didn't open for another hour but I had been putting in big miles and was very hungry and willing to wait. I was enjoying a chicken fried steak and eggs, hash browns, and pancakes when Chuckles and Chatterbox arrived. They were brother and sister hikers in their early twenties. Pretty soon, Nate and Jenna showed up. I smiled. They were as dirty as hell! When I first met them they were so squeaky clean. They both headed to the restroom to wash up while their food was cooking. When they came back they were still kind of grubby. I smiled again. Now they were thru-hikers.

After a filling breakfast I was the first to head back to the Trail. Jenna and Nate followed an hour later. Even with lack of sleep and thirty miles of hard hiking the previous day, I felt ready to tackle the day. The next fourteen miles were uphill, hot, and brutal. The hike started at 2,200 feet and ended at 7,100 feet. It was some of the thickest, healthiest forest that I hiked through. There were small, clean, streams in abundance and I was drinking from nearly every stream I crossed. It felt great to drink as much as I wanted of the cold mountain water. I passed Snow White and Mr.C while they were taking a break. They were a young couple who looked like they were being worn down by the Trail. I passed Minor two hours later while he was taking a break near the crest of a mountain. He started hiking the PCT right after graduating from high school. I was proud to make 23.5 miles and I didn't feel overly tired at the end of the day.

The next day was difficult but enjoyable hiking. I was out of the thick forest and hiking through more open spaces. Water was less abundant and I had to go one half mile off Trail to fill up. I made it to the half-way point in the afternoon. Jenna and Nate were there taking a break near the half-way marker. A couple of other hikers showed up and were excited. I felt nothing. I'm not sure why. Maybe it was because I knew I still had 1,330 miles to go. I know I hadn't focused on the half-way point as a goal. My focus was reaching Highway 70 by 5:00 pm, a hitch into Chester, California and food, a motel room, and a shower in that order. I made it to Highway 70 right at 5:00 pm. Jenna, Nate, and Maverick showed up ten minutes later. We exceeded our goal. We averaged 25.4 miles a day between Sierra city and Chester.

There was a sign at the Trailhead for southbound hikers heading to

Belden:

"The Pacific Crest Trail is closed to hikers from Chester to Belden due to forest fire." What? We had just been through that area. Apparently, we were among the last hikers to get through before the fire. Chuckles and Chatterbox didn't make it through. Neither did Snow White, Mr.C, or Minor. Minor woke up in the night and was staring into the barrel of a rifle being aimed at him by a Law Enforcement Ranger who thought he was the person who started the fire. It turned out to be one of the worst fires in California in 2012, lasting weeks and burning thousands of acres of forest. It started on the PCT about four miles north of the Belden trailhead. That was a gorgeous area. For weeks, thru-hikers behind us had to take a fire detour which was mainly a road walk. If we hadn't set a goal of 25 miles a day we would have been one of the road walkers.

Nate and Jenna gave me a chance to get the first ride since I had gotten to the highway before them. There were some hikers across the highway getting ready to continue north and they visited with them. I tried hitching for a half an hour with no luck. Finally, Nate, Jenna, and Maverick came over. Jenna always kept her hair bundled up in a bandana. She took off her bandana, shook out her red hair which came down below her shoulders, and within five minutes we had a ride. A man driving a Chevy Geo Metro stopped for us. We were desperate and the driver was willing, so we stuffed into the little car. Jenna and Nate said I deserved the front seat since I had gotten to the highway first. In the backseat, Maverick and Nate who were both over 6' tall were on the outside with Jenna in the middle. They were holding their backpacks in front of them. It was a hot day and I rolled down the window right away. As we were driving uphill and the little Geo was straining to its limit, the driver asked if we would like for him to turn on the air conditioning. We all said simultaneously: "NO!" Driving along the winding hills, I was waiting for one of the tiny tires to pop and send us rolling down the side of the mountain.

Chester was a nice little town. We were dropped off in front of the Pine Shack Frosty which seemed to be the social center of town. It had a reputation for having excellent milkshakes. There must have been thirty flavors to choose from. I ordered a peanut butter shake. It was exceptionally good. I was hot, thirsty, and hungry and it really hit the spot. The best shake I had on my thru-hike and I had a lot of them. I decided to get a motel room and clean up before having dinner. When I was taking a shower, the bandage covering my wound became so wet that it fell off. I looked at the wound. It had been ten days since I fell. There was no scabbing on it. It didn't look like it had healed at all. I cleaned it, put Neosporin on it, and attached another big bandage.

The next morning I headed to the Post Office to pick up my resupply box. When I opened it, there were new shoes. The last pair had taken me from Kennedy Meadows to Chester - 632 miles. They still looked good. I regret not sending them home. I left them in the motel room. The new Brooks Cascadia's with their thick cushioning, felt great. While I was in town I put in more than 7,000 much needed calories. I made one last stop on my way out of town and had an excellent breakfast burrito and another shake. Brit, David, and Minor were sitting at the table next to mine. I told them about the hiker who woke up to have a rifle pointed at him. Minor was paying close attention. When I finished he said: "That was me!" I stared at him: "Yea. It was, wasn't it?" Duh.

As I was eating my burrito, a couple at the next table struck up a conversation. They had a fifth wheel trailer and were camped nearby. They were curious about my thru-hike and asked a lot of questions. They saw my pack, asked if I was heading back to the Trail, and offered me a ride. I gladly accepted.

I started hiking at 1:00 pm. Nate and Jenna started an hour earlier. I knew they were going to continue to try to maintain a twenty-five miles a day pace. I decided to go back to my twenty-two miles a day pace. I had a feeling that was the last I was going to see of them. It had been fun hiking with them. I knew with their attitude and enthusiasm, they were going to have a successful thru-hike.

I hiked ten miles and stopped for the night near a bridge that crossed the Feather River. I put my tent on the same spot I camped the year before. What a difference a year made. The year before, I had been ill at ease. Sounds in the night, such as a snapping twig, startled me. I would sit up in my sleeping bag, "What was that?" waiting with my eyes wide open to hear another sound. This time I had spent over seventy nights camping alone. I was perfectly at ease in the forest. I slept undisturbed and soundly, as I did most nights.

The next morning I started early. I passed healthy, beautiful, forest and bubbling mud ponds with a strong sulfur smell. I was looking forward to reaching Drakesbad Guest Ranch by lunch. I had heard nothing but good things about Drakesbad. It was in a wide valley filled with thick, green, grasses and pines. A clear mountain stream passed nearby. Ed and Billie Fiebiger were the owners. It was a popular place and always booked solid. Here is what these kind people did for thru-hikers and it was all free: You were given a bar of soap and a fluffy towel and pointed to the showers. Your clothes were cleaned for you. You were given loaner swimming clothes so you could use their big swimming pool fed by natural hot springs. One of the things that brought guests back year after year was the quality of their food. This was what I was looking forward to. After the guests were served, it was our turn. Everything was freshly cooked and freshly baked - soups, breads, pastries, cookies. The quality of the food was superb and I went back for seconds, thirds, and fourths. I finished with cups of delicious coffee. The total came to $6.92. Drakesbad completely lived up to its reputation. Ed and Billie had nothing to gain by doing this for thru-hikers. They were just kind, generous, people and they and their friendly staff left a warm memory in my heart.

The next 230 miles from Drakesbad to Etna, California was fun, but brutal. This was the first week of August and it was hot! I hiked with Magic Bag, Mark, Minor, David, Brit, Lil Dipper, Jack y Bean, Gut Feeling, Ninja, Shack, and Weeki, We hiked along at the same rate for close to 1,000 miles.

Mark was at least 6'7" tall. I always knew when he was ahead of me. I would see his size 14 Cascadia 7 shoe prints. I could place my shoe over his shoe print and there would be a five inch overlap. Minor started hiking the PCT ten days after I started. He was hiking with Mark, Magic Bag, Brit, and David. He was capable of huge miles and by Washington had left everyone in the dust. David and Brit had hiked together from the start and were fit and fast. Lil Dipper and Jack y Bean were a young couple and Gut Feeling had hiked with them from the start. They were intelligent, educated, and verbal. Most of the time they hiked together and always had a conversation going. I wish I had made more of an effort to get to know them. Ninja was a true character. Non-stop verbal. I liked him. I think he was one of the most social people I met on my hike. He knew how to party and was enjoying every minute of his thru-hike. He had instant recall of the trail name of every hiker he met. By the time I got to know him he had already taken twenty-four zero's and we still had over 1,000 miles left to get to Canada. The guy could put in thirty-five mile days and be finished by 6:00 pm. Disgusting! Shack and Weeki helped make my hike the joy that it was. They were from New Zealand. Shack was fifty-seven and his son, Weeki (short for wee-kiwi) was eighteen. It took a while to get acquainted but we leapfrogged all the way to Canada. It was always a pleasure to stop and chat on the Trail or visit with them in Trail towns.

Leaving Drakesbad, there was a steep, switch backed climb that was dreadful. I was fuller than a tick. I just wanted to take a nap. Pretty soon the coffee and all the cookies and cake kicked in and I got going. I passed Kings Creek where I ended my hike a year earlier. The water was still moving rapidly, but manageable. I was in Lassen Volcanic National Park and there were great views of glacier covered Mt. Lassen.

The next day I was going to hike Hat Creek Rim. Since I started planning my hike months earlier it had stood out as a major challenge and I was looking forward to it. There was no natural on-trail water for the next 33.5 miles and it was supposed to be extremely HOT. I headed to Old Station to take extra liquid for the 33.5 mile waterless stretch. Old Station was 3/10th of a mile from the Trail and was tiny, but it had a Chevron with a mini-mart. I had my four regular quart bottles of water and added two quart bottles of cranberry juice. That was a good choice which I used quite a few times to the end of my hike. I would dilute the tart cranberry juice with my regular water and it added an interesting variety. The Chevron had brand new owners, a husband and wife, who had been on the job for less than two weeks. He was helpful, she was super-enthusiastic. She had me sign a thru-hiker guest book, took my picture and put it on a bulletin board along with pictures of dozens of other thru-hikers. She was bubbling with energy and eagerness to build her business. I'll bet she does, too.

Back on the Trail, the hiking was gentle for the first mile. Ahead, I could see a sheer wall over a hundred feet high that continued as far as I could see. The pathway up the wall was switch backed and steep. I finally made it to the rim but I was sweating heavily in the morning heat. I remember thinking: "If this is what it feels like in the morning, what is it going to feel like in the afternoon after I have been hiking for hours?" I had eaten two huge beef and bean burritos while I was at the Chevron. Each burrito was 900 calories and had more than a day's worth of salt. I should have cameled up with water before leaving and I was feeling super thirsty. Four miles into the hike I stopped at a highway overlook and saw the parents of Stonewall. Stonewall and I had lunch together at Drakesbad and he introduced me to his parents when we were at the Chevron. I waved at them. Stonewall's mother came over and handed me two, sixteen ounce bottles of Gatorade. Talk about trail magic. I chugged them on the spot and put the empty bottles in my pack.

The area next to the pathway along Hat Creek Rim was barren for miles. A forest fire many years ago left the area almost treeless. The landscape was covered with cactus, and dry, brown, native grasses. The pathway was a combination of dirt and volcanic rock. I kicked up a lot of dust as I hiked. The views were vast and impressive. It was fun walking along the rim with its steep drop-offs, for hours at a time. There were a few old juniper and cypress trees next to the rim that survived previous fires. They made excellent shady spots to take a break, eat some food, and enjoy the magnificent views. From the rim I was looking down on everything.

While I was hiking I was completely exposed to the hot sun. It felt like I was back in the desert and I started rationing my water again. I had thirty-three miles to the next water source and six quarts of water. I figured a quart should last six miles. I could hike pretty fast on the relatively flat Trail, so I estimated a three miles per hour hiking speed. That allowed me to drink a quart every two hours. I would spread the quart out and not drink any large quantities all at once although I was dying to. There was supposed to be a water cache eighteen miles into the hike but I couldn't count on it. It stayed hot into the evening. By 8:00 pm I found a camping spot in a grove of cypress. Stonewall joined me a half an hour later. Many thru-hikers hiked Hat Creek Rim in the cool of the night and I heard three groups pass by in the night.

I started early the next morning while it was still relatively cool. The water cache was in nine miles and I reached it by 11:00 am. It had gallons of water in the shade of a big tree. I even met the Trail Angel who kept the gallon jugs filled. I personally thanked him. I always wanted to do that. I drank close to two quarts of water on the spot and topped off my water bottles. I even filled the two extra 16 ounce Gatorade bottles. I was carrying fourteen pounds of water to hike the next fifteen, hot, hot, miles. It felt good not to hold back when I was really thirsty and to completely slake my thirst. It felt good to drink down the water weight, too. This day was harder than the previous one. Eventually the Trail led down from the rim over big areas of lava. The footing over the lava rock was sharp and uneven. I slowed way down. A fall would have cut me to pieces. The sun was pounding and two days of hiking over lava rock left my feet tender. I could feel every rock.

Fortunately I had a new pair of shoes. I passed David, whose shoes were worn and almost tread less. He looked in agony as he slowly made his way along the Trail. I hiked into the evening until I reached the trees. I stopped a mile short of the water source. I had a quart of water left and found a shady spot in a field to put my tent. I was tired after two, grueling, twenty-two mile days and slept for ten hours. It felt good to be out of the intense heat of Hat Creek Rim and back into the trees.

I spent a lot of the next day hiking near water. I passed the Crystal Lake Fish Hatchery, Baum Lake, Lake Britton and Burney Falls, before climbing into thick forest. I spent the afternoon hiking along the sides of mountains. I saw Mt. Shasta for the first time. It was far in distance and huge. It stayed in view and I would see it from different angles for the next twelve days.

I hiked a total of twenty-seven miles. It was more than I planned but for the last ten miles I couldn't find a camping spot. I put up my tent in the dark. I knew I was close to a water source but I didn't realize how close. The next morning I walked downhill about thirty yards and there was a small stream. Nine hikers were just beginning their day. They camped next to the stream the night before. I talked to Shack and Weeki for the first time. We stayed at the same motel when we were in Bridgeport and had eaten at the same restaurant. We nodded to each other. We stayed at the same motel in Chester and had eaten at the same restaurant, but again we just nodded to one another. The stream had slowly flowing water and was almost stagnant. I needed water badly so I filled my water bottles at the same spot as all nine people before me. Shack was standing behind me when I finished. With his New Zealand accent he said: "Geed Woata." I nodded in agreement although I wasn't convinced. Weeki came over and introduced himself and his father.

This was a hot hiking day with long distances between water. Later in the day I met Shack and Weeki near a little spring while they were taking a break. The ice cold water was gushing. Shack greeted me with: "Great Woata." It was. I sat with them and chatted a few minutes. We leapfrogged for much of the day.

The previous three days had been difficult hiking. The first two days had been extremely hot stretches. I pushed the pace to get through them and although I had been drinking a lot of water I had been losing hydration. The third day was twenty-seven difficult miles in the early August heat. In the afternoon, after a hot climb, I took a piss and my urine was Bright Red! I was three days from a highway or I would have gone immediately to a hospital. I was on the verge of panic but remembered listening to a good marathoner who talked about having blood in his urine after a hard training session without enough water. The next water source was half a mile away. When I reached it, I drank two quarts on the spot. I filled my water bottles and drank every ten minutes as I continued to hike. I started to feel a little bloated and probably overcompensated. The next time I pissed it was dark yellow with blood in it. I kept drinking more water. Pretty soon I was pissing every ten minutes. The urine became lighter shades of yellow until eventually it became clear. That scared the hell out of me. Fortunately, water sources were becoming more abundant so I was able to stay well hydrated - And I Did!

Later in the day I saw a big cinnamon colored bear that went crashing through the woods when it saw me. Bears are fast. Most people don't realize how fast they are. I camped in a pine forest thick with vegetation. I heard a loud, crashing sound about 3:00 am. Ninja, who was camped nearby, said he saw a bear in the night.

There was a water source one half mile from the Trail. I really didn't want to go that far but with the red urine weighing heavily on my mind, I decided to fill up. I was taking down my tent when Weeki and Shack passed. They needed to get water and headed down. By the time I was packed and ready to hike, they were back. Shack said: "Geed Woata." By this time I had figured out how to differentiate between "Geed Woata" and "Great Woata". I was thinking: "Oh, Oh." I left my fully loaded backpack next to the Trail and just took the water bottles down to the water source. I hiked through an area heavy with vegetation. There were bright flowers everywhere. I noticed something else. There were bear droppings everywhere. I needed water so I kept going. The water source was a twenty foot pool supplied by a barely moving stream. There was only one small area where I could get water and it had a wide worn spot that was used by the bear to drink. I still needed water and filled up. I should have used my Aqua Mira drops but I didn't. Heading back to the Trail it occurred to me that my backpack, which was full of food, was unguarded and there was a bear in the area. I anxiously trotted back to my pack. It was untouched.

It was a beautiful day of hiking through pine forests with many high mountain views. I hiked until it was nearly dark, trying to find a place to camp. I passed a beautiful spot by a stream but three hikers were sitting next to it and I thought they had claimed it. I continued on. I couldn't find any place to put a tent and the next water source was miles ahead so I headed back. There was a small area across the stream level enough to put a tent. It was pretty rough. It didn't look like it had ever been used. As I was putting up my tent I felt something sting my leg. Then I felt another sting, then another. I continued putting up the tent as fast as I could and hopped in. Tiny hornets were coming out of their nest on the ground. I didn't have time to stake the tent. The outer cover was leaning against the netting and there was no ventilation. I checked to see where I had been bitten. There were ten stings on my legs and arms creating little bumps that itched for the next two days. Right about this time the three hikers passed my tent. They had only been taking a break and were heading out for a night hike. How thoughtless! They knew I was looking for a camping spot and should have offered it. I realized I couldn't spend the night like this. I waited for the hornets to calm down, quickly got out of the tent and carried it twenty yards away. I was stung a couple of more times and was pissed!

Much of the next day was uphill climbing. It was in an area full of shady trees. There were small streams and water was plentiful. It was an enjoyable day of hiking. Since leaving Chester a week earlier I was still having trouble with the wound on my right arm. The central area wasn't healing. The wound was creating a lot of pus that leaked out of the edges of the bandage. By the end of the day the pus was thick and hardened. Usually I would clean it off but I decided to leave it alone to see what would happen. After two days there was a thick scab circling the outside of the bandage. It was gross and I got a lot of concerned comments on it. I cleaned it off and from then on continued to clean off the pus at the end of the day. It was a hot day and I was grateful for the shady trees. There were long, tiring climbs. When I passed streams I would see hikers sprawled out in camping spots taking naps. I caught up to Mark, Magic Bag, Brit, David, and Minor. They found a pool of water deep enough to jump into. I was tempted to join them but didn't want to contaminate my wound. I hiked through an area that had been logged and crossed a number of old dirt logging roads. Toward the end of the day I took a break on an old logging road that hadn't been used in years. There was an extra wide area on a curve that looked like it could accommodate a lot of campers. There was even a well-used fire ring. It looked like a popular destination for hikers. It was on a mountaintop. The sun was just starting to set and small clouds in the distance were turning crimson. I finished my break and headed on. Within fifty yards I found a great spot to camp. Over the next two hours I listened as the camping area on the old logging road filled up. Magic Bag, Ninja, Mark, David, Brit, Minor, Chuckles, Chatterbox, Lil Dipper, Jack y Bean, and Gut Feeling showed up. There was no loud partying. They had put in a full day. They had a fire going and quietly chatted while they cooked their dinner.

The next morning there was a four mile downhill hike to a highway and two more miles to a Chevron station that had a deli and enough food for a resupply. I started hiking by 7:00 am. Every hiker that I mentioned started before me. The younger hikers took a lot more zeros than I did but when they were hiking they didn't mind putting in the hours. Our hiking styles were very different but we all consistently averaged twenty-two miles a day and stayed together well into Washington.

My hiking style or strategy was to hike at a steady pace staying well within my ability. A steady pace would allow me to hike between twenty and twenty-eight miles a day. I wasn't looking for thirty mile days. I only had three days of thirty plus miles. I rarely went all out, figuring that going too fast, in the long run, would wear me out and possibly cause injury. If I didn't overexert and wear down, I wouldn't need to take a lot of zero days to recover. I took seven zero's the whole trip.

A good night's sleep was very important to me. It allowed me to recharge my weary body. I always slept in a tent, screened from insects, and on a comfortable air mattress. I slept eight to ten hours each night but if I was really tired I could sleep up to twelve hours. I never set an alarm or forced myself to get up early. I always slept until I was ready to get up. I could be completely dragging before going to bed but after a good night's sleep, I would be raring to go the next morning.

I would try to hike from 7:30 am to 7:30 pm each day. If I slept in late and didn't get started until 8:00 am, then I would hike until 8:00 pm. During the end of June and all of July and August when it stayed daylight until 8:30 pm, I would hike almost until dark if I wanted to put in bigger miles or if I was on the side of a mountain and couldn't find a level camping spot. Most times I was more than happy, even eager, to stop by 7:30 pm and would be checking my watch and looking for a spot to put my tent. Only ten times did I hike into darkness and only once intentionally.

I took food breaks every two hours. This kept a constant supply of fuel in my system and a steady flow of energy. I mainly ate trail mix but would supplement it with anything I found appetizing when I resupplied. The fifteen minute breaks every two hours gave me a chance to rest. I would find a soft spot in the dirt next to the Trail and lie down on my side while I ate. This took pressure off of my back and was comfortable. The only drawback was having so much of my body on the ground. There were always ants anywhere I stopped and I was bitten a lot of times. I tried to start the day with a lot of calories. Breakfast might be two bagels with a heavy layer of Nutella and two pop tarts. That would be about 1,200 calories. Dinner was usually just before going to sleep and was as much trail mix as I could eat. After a long day it could be a massive amount. Fortunately I liked the stuff. Total breaks in a twelve hour hiking day would be between one and a half and two hours. The time I was actually hiking each day was a minimum of ten solid hours.

My pace varied with the Trail conditions. If the Trail had good footing I would try to keep a pace of at least three miles per hour. If the Trail was rocky and uneven I would hike between two and two and a half miles per hour. If the Trail was difficult and I was hiking on steep down hills with small, loose rocks, I would go the speed it would take to hike safely - sometimes one mile per hour. There would be days where the hiking was difficult all day. Those were the days I would hike from 7:30 am to 8:30 pm and only make twenty miles. I think overall, I averaged a 2.5 mph pace.

My plan for hiking the Pacific Crest Trail was a good plan. No..... It was a great plan! As a sixty-five year old hiker, I hiked the 2,660 mile Pacific Crest Trail in one hundred and forty-nine days. I hiked at a steady pace, staying well within my ability. I was never sick or even had an upset stomach. I never needed or took an aspirin or Ibuprofen. The only thing that slowed me down was the broken tooth.

When I started my hike I tried to share my hiking plan with the fervor of a true believer. To me it was so simple so logical so right! I tried quite a few times. I was met with indifference. After a while I said: "Screw it! Let them find their own way."

There didn't seem to be any logic in the way many young people hiked. They had amazing stamina and endurance. They could start at daybreak and hike far into the night. A lot of them cowboy camped which saved putting up and taking down a tent and made for a quick start in the morning. They loved to night hike and spent many nights doing it. Night hiking really messes up your sleep schedule. They would have big bags under their eyes the next day. They hiked fast which allowed them to swim if they found a good lake or stream, or head down to a resort a few miles off Trail for a cheeseburger and shake. They did that frequently and still put in thirty plus mile days. I was always watching them pay for their exuberance. They would string these incredibly long, tiring, days together until they hit a town and would be totally exhausted. They would have nasty blisters and sore muscles from all the overuse and have to spend extra days in town to recover. That was probably part of the plan. They thoroughly enjoyed their zero days.

I made it to the Chevron before noon. I had two good breakfast burritos stuffed with salsa, ham and egg, a freshly made ham sandwich, two fruit salads, a pint of Ben and Jerry's ice cream and four big chocolate chip cookies. I ate way too much. There was a little shady, grassy, spot for hikers in front of the Chevron where we all gathered. The resupply was atrocious and expensive.

I headed back to the Trail by 1:00 pm. When I reached the Trailhead and started heading north, I was full and lethargic. I was going to be climbing continuously for the next eighteen miles in the Castle Crags Wilderness. Castle Crag Mountain was on the right of the Trail with its sheer, craggy, cliffs. It was impressive. The hiking was rocky and steeply uphill, with a lot of switch-backs. I was moving slowly and was passed by Mark, Brit, and David. They had passed me so many times in the last few days they hardly acknowledged me. My mind said: "OK. That's enough. I'm tired of this!" For the next sixteen miles I went full out. All the food energy kicked in and I only stopped once, just long enough to drink some water. Mark had a sore foot and was easy to pass. David and Brit were in excellent condition, saw me catching up to them, and picked up the pace. Mile after mile, non-stop, I was very gradually catching up to them. Eventually I was only twenty feet behind David and would jam my hiking stick down to get traction and let him know I was catching him. I stayed twenty feet behind for another half mile. Now the gap was down to ten feet. He stopped to take a picture. HA! Gotcha! I nodded as I passed. Brit was thirty yards ahead. By now I was totally into the game. I was jamming my hiking stick down and hiking at top speed. So much adrenaline was flowing, I didn't feel tired. I was getting closer. I was within twenty feet and Brit decided to stop and take in the view. HA! I was panting from the continuous effort but before I passed Brit I took a deep breath, slowly exhaled, and said casually: "It's kind of breezy, isn't it?" It sounded like I wasn't breathing hard at all. I continued at the same pace for the next hour. I finally stopped at a tiny spring surrounded by ferns and small, delicate flowers. A doe was grazing in the grassy meadow. David and Brit caught up just as I was leaving. They were in a good mood. I think they enjoyed the game. I was to see them many more times on the Trail. From then on they would go out of their way to stop and talk.

It was 8:30 pm by the time I found a spot to put my tent. I had to drop down a steep ten foot embankment to get there. The camping area was only about ten feet wide and fifteen feet long. It was completely surrounded by a four foot tall bush with thick, dark green leaves, and shiny branches that looked like teak. The whole mountainside was covered by this bush. It was dark by the time I had my tent set up. Brit and David passed with their headlamps on. They weren't the least bit concerned to be hiking late into the night. It was a great spot to put my tent. It was peaceful and quiet. There was a slight breeze rustling the leaves. I was sound asleep in no time. As I was taking down the tent the next morning I noticed about the biggest bear dump I had seen in my life. It was five feet from my tent. I breathed a big sigh of relief I hadn't seen it as I was putting up the tent the night before. I would have had owl eyes all night long.

The next day captured the beauty of the Pacific Crest Trail that I loved.

It was spent almost completely above tree line. The path was smooth and well maintained. I could see the pathway miles in the distance as it wound around the sides of mountains. Often, the area next to the Trail was covered with scrub oak. I spent most of the day high on the mountain looking down on sparkling lakes. Sometimes the Trail would head down to a lake and then head way back to the top. The views were unlimited. The cloudless sky was a bright blue.

High on the mountain, I stopped and talked with volunteer Trail maintainers clearing the encroaching vegetation. There were four of them. They were tanned and fit and putting a lot of effort into the hard work. All of them were in their sixties. As we talked, I could sense the easy camaraderie of good friends. I thanked them for the work they were doing. They made hiking safer, more enjoyable, and stabilized the Trail which could deteriorate fast if not maintained.

I looked at my bandaged right arm for confirmation. Maintaining the Pacific Crest Trail kept them fit, allowed them to be outdoors in beautiful country, and gave them the pride of accomplishment. It gave them a sense of purpose.

One of the benefits of hiking solo was that it gave me hours of time alone with my thoughts. This helped me define what is important to me. One thing I realized was that I need a sense of purpose. For a few years I helped my next door neighbor, Joyce, who had been recently widowed. I took care of her yard, and before she moved to California, helped her with yard sales and to clean up her house. She repaid me with some really good home cooking, but she didn't have to. It felt good to be helpful. She thanked me for my efforts. That felt good, too. I have found that doing something productive with no other motive than to be helpful, is rewarding.

I take my dog, Fred, for a walk each morning to the nearby park. I noticed a lot of dog droppings and trash on the ground. Sometimes it would stay there for days. After I returned from my PCT hike, I began picking it up. If it wasn't grass, bark, or twigs, I picked it up, no matter how small. Now, the park looks pretty good. Each day I still find dog droppings and trash that I put it into a plastic grocery bag and into a trash receptacle. No one knows I do this. It feels good to see a clean park. For such a small amount of effort, it gives me a lot of satisfaction.

I spent the next two days hiking high on mountains with gorgeous views. I put in twenty-three and twenty-nine mile days before stopping six miles short of the road to Etna, California. Etna had always been a goal of mine, not only because it had a reputation as one of the best Trail towns, but the name Etna. Doug, his wife, Ingrid, and daughter, Karin, live in Etna, New Hampshire and I was eager to give them a phone call: "You'll never guess where I'm calling from....." When I did call, Karin sounded surprised. Thank you, Karin.

Etna was right up there with Sierra City, in my book, as a great Trail town. It was a small mountain town with a friendly, relaxed atmosphere. It only had one motel which was full. There weren't any cars in front of it so it must have been filled with thru-hikers. I was disappointed. The only alternative was the Hiker Hut at Alderbrook Manor. It was a hostel on the edge of town. I reluctantly headed to the hostel, grumbling under my breath. Alderbrook Manor was an impressive turn-of-the-century house and one of the biggest houses in town. It was also an expensive bed and breakfast. It had beautifully maintained flower gardens, a koi pond with flowing fountain, and thick green grass on a one acre yard. The Hiker Hut Hostel consisted of a couple of travel trailers converted to bunk space and a bunk room with six bunks. The bunk room had a computer, TV with VCR, a selection of movies, and a bathroom with a shower. The place was teeming with thru-hikers. The owner, Vicki, told me there was one more bunk bed left for twenty-five dollars. I was inwardly groaning. This was a small, confining area. I saw the thick green grass in the spacious back yard and asked if I could put up a tent back there. "Sure." She only charged me ten dollars and I had use of the shower and other amenities. I was the first to put up my tent and put it near the fountain. Other hikers began filling the back yard with their tents and by nightfall there were at least seventeen tents on the lawn.

There was only one shower and tons of people so I headed to Bob's Ranch House for breakfast and took a seat at the counter. The waitress greeted me with a pleasant smile. There were fifteen other people having breakfast and the waitress, who was the only one on duty, was handling it easily. There was a man sitting at the counter next to the register who looked to be in his seventies. Customers would come over and chat with him. I figured that was Bob. He was probably retired and enjoyed being around the restaurant he had started. Another waitress showed up. It started to get busy. Having been in the restaurant business when I was in my mid-twenties, I can't help but be constantly judging restaurants where I eat. It was a pleasure to watch the people in this restaurant in action. Bob headed to the grill. The cook, who had been working the grill, moved to the side and started making pancakes and hash browns. Now the restaurant was nearly full. My waitress was in constant motion as she was seating customers, taking orders, giving them to Bob, refilling coffee cups, taking food to customers, cleaning the counter and tables when customers left, putting clean silverware back on the tables, and ringing up customers who were paying their bill. All of this would have overwhelmed an average waitress. Her timing was perfect. She knew exactly what to give priority to. (From a manager's perspective, that is so hard to teach.) I had my food in minutes. It was hot, fresh, and bountiful. The price was reasonable, but not cheap. (Bob knew how to make a profit.) Bob was moving fast but totally in control. He was dinging his little "Order Up" bell about every two minutes. The waitresses would be right on it. Bob and the waitresses were at the top of their game. I like watching the best and they were the best. I gave my waitress a five dollar tip. She earned it. I had a feeling she made a good living. There were only two waitresses, Bob, and the other cook. Orders were taken quickly, the food was cooked to order, on the table in a surprisingly short time, and delicious. I had dinner and two breakfasts there. It cost sixty dollars and was worth every penny.

While I was at the counter waiting for my food, Magic Bag, who had just finished his breakfast, came over to talk. His ankle was badly swollen and he was limping. He told me he was going to stay at the hostel for a few days to see if it would recover, but it wasn't looking good. He said he had made peace with the fact that he might have to end his hike. He said if he didn't see me again, it had been a pleasure hiking with me. "When I first met you just before Sierra City, Jim, I thought: "I'll pass this older guy after Sierra City and never see him again." But then I kept passing you over and over. You are fast!"

I didn't follow the logic, but I did appreciate the thought.

It was a disappointment to hear Magic Bag might be leaving the Trail. It was obvious he was enjoying his thru-hike immensely. I wished him luck and told him how much I enjoyed hiking with him. Just before he left, I told him I had a feeling he would soon be zipping by me like he always did. Although he sounded pretty confident he was through, I didn't buy it. I had seen plenty of hikers on the Appalachian Trail and Pacific Crest Trail I was pretty sure would quit. I didn't see any quit in Magic Bag.

After breakfast I headed back to Hiker Haven. I took a long needed shower. The bandage came off as I was cleaning my arm. It hadn't been off since I had a shower fourteen days earlier in Chester. I gasped. It had been twenty-three days since I had fallen. I couldn't believe it. The main part of the wound hadn't healed at all. It was an angry red and slightly bulging. I cleaned it gently and thoroughly. It was now obvious it wasn't going to heal on its own. I needed to find out how to treat it. Hikers inside the bunkroom were examining the wound and were repulsed. Call it fate. Call it luck. Call it anything you want. In the morning, as David, Brit, Mark, and I were waiting to hitch into town another hiker came off of the Trail to join us. His name was Ben. In passing, I heard Mark mention that he was a doctor. Ben wasn't even staying at the hostel. He was staying at the Bed and Breakfast. He came down to visit a couple of people he had been hiking with. He was standing next to me so I asked him if he would look at my arm. He was an emergency room physician. He very calmly and clinically analyzed the wound.

"Gently clean it each day with a wet gauze pad. Keep it clean and cover it with a bandage that gives it plenty of air to breathe. Stop using Neosporin on it. It looks like that has caused redness. I have some extra bandages if you need them."

I gratefully thanked him. I headed to the grocery store to resupply and bought plenty of small gauze pads and big roomy bandages. Each morning before getting out of my sleeping bag, I would take a fresh gauze pad, pour a little water into the cap of my water bottle, soak the pad, tear off the old bandage, gently clean the wound, and put on a fresh bandage. The progress was immediate. It was a big relief watching a new layer of skin grow. Within two weeks I no longer needed a bandage. It left a scar on my arm that almost looks like a tattoo.

I didn't think I would but I enjoyed my stay at the Hiker Haven. One time was plenty, but I could see how this would be enjoyable for other hikers. I met hikers I hadn't seen in ages. Sprinkles who I had last seen 1,340 miles earlier, had a ride back to the Trail and was just heading out. It was good to see him again. Lightweight was still as thin as ever but now had a full beard. I had last seen him 900 miles earlier at Kennedy Meadows. He remarked that the last time he saw me I had a beard (I was clean shaven since my visit with the Pryor's) and I pointed out the last time I saw him he hadn't had one. We talked about people we had hiked with. Most of them had left the Trail. Lightweight was totally in his element as a thru-hiker. I had a feeling his transition back to the "real world" after his thru-hike was going to be a rough one.

Weeki, Shack, Magic Bag, Brit, David, Minor, Mark, Gut Feeling, Jack y Bean and Lil Dipper were all there. I met hikers I would hike with or around for hundreds of miles: Turtle and Willilly, Baro and H Bomb, Spatula, Mismatch, Pit Stop, Knees, Body Bag, and Freestyle.

Turtle and Willilly, a young couple from the Netherlands, passed me just thirty miles before Canada. Knees, Freestyle, and Body Bag, finished their thru-hike hours after me. There were so many new people and names to remember, it was overwhelming.

After resupplying at the grocery store, I came back and organized my food in the shade of a giant oak tree. I was sitting on thick, soft, grass. Shack and Weeki joined me and we got a good conversation going. Other hikers joined us. The talk for the next couple of hours was hiker talk and I enjoyed being part of it.

It was difficult trying to get to sleep that night. We were right next to the main road leading into town and cars were loud as they passed by. We were in a neighborhood and a party was going on in one of the houses. Dogs were barking.

I even listened to a dog fight. There was a band playing at a nearby park. It was a big event for the little town. I was trying to get to sleep and was irritated by the distractions. I decided to relax, enjoy the sounds, and forget about trying to sleep. It turned into a pleasant memory. The band was playing songs from my era and I would hum along. It was kind of nostalgic.

After an enjoyable stay in Etna, I hitch hiked back to the Trail and was hiking by 11:00 am. This was difficult, rocky, hiking and my feet ached at the end of the day.

This is when I first started noticing the smoke from fires. It was a bad season for forest fires in California, Oregon, and Washington. From this day (August 12th) until the end of my thru-hike, I was constantly dealing with the effects of forest fires.

Long distance views were often hazy and the smell of smoke was in the air. There were days when the smoke made it difficult to breathe. Sometimes there were huge plumes of smoke coming up from the other side of a mountain and the Trail was heading in that direction. It caused anxiety. Mountain ranges that were supposed to be spectacular were shrouded in smoke. I rarely used my camera in Oregon and Washington. The threat of Trail closure was always there.

I passed Freestyle and Body Bag who were taking a swim in a lake. It was a hot day and the clear, blue, water looked tempting but I needed to keep my wound clean. I started looking for a camping spot by 7:00 pm. It was almost 9:00 pm before I found one. Cattle were allowed to graze in the section that the Trail passed through. Their grazing churned up the ground for miles. I found a spot that wasn't great but I was getting desperate. I heard cowbells nearby and kept going.

About 8:45 pm I was passed by Freestyle and Body Bag. I whined about my frustration at not being able to find a good camping spot. Ten minutes later Freestyle and Body Bag were seated next to an absolutely perfect spot that was smooth and flat with gorgeous views. Inwardly I was saying: "This would have been perfect." When I caught up to them I gave a little, forced smile. That was what they were waiting for. They burst out laughing. They had no intention of tenting there for the night and were just waiting for my reaction. It was given in good humor and taken in good humor. We all had a good laugh and I had a beautiful campsite. It was dark as I set up the tent. I was passed by Mark, David, and Brit. They stopped briefly to chat. Ben passed ten minutes later with his headlamp shining. Once I was in my sleeping bag and getting ready to sleep, Gut Feeling stopped and chatted. Most were headed to a forest service cabin which was their arranged destination for the night. It was five miles up the Trail. They would get there between 10:30 pm and 11:00 pm but that didn't bother them at all.

I am going to take you through one day of the 149 days of my thru-hike:

It took about a month to get into a really solid routine. Once I did, it made my hike much more enjoyable. I would usually wake up between 6:00 am and 6:30 am. It took between an hour and an hour and fifteen minutes to start hiking. It was usually chilly and sometimes cold in the morning. I would stay in my sleeping bag as I completely emptied my backpack. First, I would open the big orange food sack. Breakfast this day was two cinnamon bagels covered heavily with Nutella and two cinnamon pop tarts - about 1,200 calories. I would stay in my sleeping bag as I had breakfast. After breakfast, I cleaned and bandaged my wound. While still in the sleeping bag, I would change from my sleeping clothes to my regular hiking clothes. This morning I added my wind jacket and gloves for extra warmth. Some mornings it took extra will power getting out of my warm sleeping bag and there would be sincere feelings of self-pity.

I had six stuff sacks of various sizes that everything went into. There were two red sacks, an orange sack, a blue sack, green sack, and black sack. Each item in the tent went into its designated sack in the exact order. Once I had that memorized I knew at all times exactly where everything was. Need the nail clippers? Go to the heavier red bag. Once the tent was put into its sack I would load the backpack. I loaded it exactly the same way each time. I would push each sack tightly down into the backpack and end with the food sack on top. That allowed me to get to the food easily when I took a break. Finally, I would tightly secure the pack. In my left shorts pocket I had my clear plastic waterproof fisherman's wallet and Halfmile's maps that I would need for the day. In the right pocket I had my GPS. Each morning I would start hiking at a slow to moderate pace, gradually letting my muscles warm up. Often I would be hiking up to speed before I realized it. It was cool out. I was wearing my gloves and wind jacket and grateful for the warmth. My body slowly began to warm and I started to lose the feeling of being too chilly. I watched the sun rise and it was extra colorful because of the smoke from forest fires. Hiking in the early morning was an enjoyable part of the day for me. There was an anticipation of what the day would bring and being a morning person, I was wide awake and fresh. Birds were chirping in the trees. I would run into spider webs spun across the Trail during the night. Sometimes they would hit my face and cling there until I pulled them off. Once in a while they would come with the spider who seemed just as startled as I was, and as eager to be rid of me as I was of it. Each morning I looked forward to the pleasure of walking into the first rays of sunlight. Once the sunshine hit my body, I would stop, turn toward it, take off my hat, tilt my head up, and feel its warmth. Usually around 8:00 am, nature called. I would find an area in the trees, at least thirty feet from the Trail. I always took my backpack with me. Most people would drop their pack next to the Trail and head off into the woods. Whenever I saw an unoccupied pack I looked straight ahead and kept moving. I looked for a spot with loose soil next to a sturdy tree. With my heel I would kick a four inch hole leaving the loosened soil piled to the side. When I was finished I would cover the spot with the loose soil and make it look like no one had been there. A good cleaning of the hands with Purell and I was on my way.

This day was an exception. Each day I ate between 4,000 and 7,000 calories. I deliberately chose foods that were high in fiber, like Shreaded Wheat Squares and Shreaded Wheat Squares with Bran. Overall it was a good decision but once in a while it would catch up to me. Sometimes I would be hiking in the early morning and the need to get off the Trail and find relief was urgent. I would look for a good spot. The forest would be too dense with underbrush or too steep or there would be meadows or areas with small rocks I couldn't hide behind. The need would become more and more urgent until it was almost painful. I would clench my teeth and sometimes have to stop and wait for the pain in my intestines to ease. Sweat would break out on my forehead. As I was hiking rapidly and urgently I was totally focused on finding a spot with at least some privacy. Eventually I would find a spot. There were five times when I didn't. This morning was one of those times. Twenty feet from where I camped and beside a log next to the Trail was the only spot I could find. It would have been extremely embarrassing for everyone involved if hikers had come by. Fortunately, no one did.

I hiked through the Marble Mountains the day before and they had been very rocky. I was continuing through the Marble Mountains for a good part of this day. So far the hiking was pleasant. I passed a turnoff to a spring. I still had two quarts of water and didn't want to go 3/10th of a mile downhill for more. The forest service cabin was less than two hours away and I planned to take my first break there.

I came to an area that was all rocks. If I looked uphill or downhill I was looking at nothing but rocks of all sizes. It was tricky working my way over the loose rocks. I slowed way down. It took total concentration to make sure I didn't twist an ankle. Those rocky areas could be twenty feet long to over half a mile. Almost every day I would pass through them.

I reached the forest service cabin just before 10:00 am. It was in a picture perfect setting. I could see why the hikers made this a destination to stop for the night. The cabin was on the edge of a one hundred yard wide meadow full of thick, green grass and wildflowers. The meadow was surrounded by tall ponderosa pines. Under the pines were smoothed out camping spaces. There was a fire ring nearby. The old cabin looked idyllic until I saw all the mouse droppings around it. There was a creek nearby. I dropped my pack next to one of the camping spots and headed down to fill my water bottles. It was hard to get to the stream and I had to work my way through uneven grass up to my knees to get there. There wasn't much flow and I searched for a place deep enough to fill the bottles without stirring up the silt. I got down on my knees in the wet grass and reached way down to get to the water. It was worth the effort. The water in my bottles was cold and clear. I headed back to the camping spot. The day was starting to get warm and the shade felt good. As I was eating my trail mix, a little doe and her fawn walked into the meadow and started grazing on the grass. They were less than twenty feet away. They completely ignored me. It was fun watching the little fawn. It would jump straight up into the air for the sheer joy of it. A butterfly fluttered by and startled it. It followed the butterfly closely with its eyes. The world was a fascinating place.

I finished my trail mix and opened a chocolate chip Cliff Bar. I moved closer and sat on a fallen tree. I was within ten feet of the doe. A small bee came over to check me out. It slowly buzzed around getting too close for comfort and eventually settled on my arm. I gently brushed it away. It came back and didn't leave when I attempted to brush it away the second time. I didn't expect this. Usually gently brushing them away a couple of times was all it took to get them to move on. I had seen people lose their cool around bees, start frantically flailing at them and get stung. I tried again to gently brush it off to no effect. I took my hat off to use to pop it if I had to, brushed it off more aggressively and walked away from where I was standing. The bee followed. I was getting ready to pop it when it flew away.

I continued on my hike. This was a great day. Within an hour, I was high on the side of a craggy mountain. I hiked through a giant meadow that went almost to the top of the mountain and descended to a small lake deep in the valley. The meadow was filled with a rainbow of colorful flowers. Looking up through this beauty to the granite peak outlined against a deep blue sky, I stopped to enjoy it.

I passed fragrant flowers, buzzing bees, and small streams with muddy crossings. A lot of times around vegetation there would be flies. It felt like I was invading their territory and was irresistible. A fly would buzz by: Sniff. "Aaahh! A stinky hiker. What an intoxicating aroma! I think I will pursue him. There's Pierre, Emily, Jacques and Clarice. Look, Gang! Hiker Trash!" -- bbbbzzzznnnn. "Damn, flies!" I found if I kept up a good pace and kept brushing them away, I would eventually lose them. At least once a day there would be a fly about four times the size of a normal fly and about four times as loud. Its territory was only a hundred yards but in that time it would circle and make numerous passes, coming so close it would sometimes brush my arms and legs.

Eventually I headed back into the forest. I passed a lovely lake and Body Bag and Freestyle were taking a nap in their tents. They had taken a swim earlier. I continued on. The Trail headed high into the mountains. I found a spot in a shaded area near the top to take a break. It was smooth and free of roots and rocks. I took off my pack, looked for a spot free of vegetation, and leaned it against the uphill embankment beside the Trail. As I was eating my food, I was leaning on my side with most of my body draped across the Trail. This was how I usually took a break. It was quick, convenient, and comfortable. If hikers came by I could swivel to the side or stand up to let them pass. Often as I was taking a break there were ants around. I never tired of watching their industriousness. There was a pattern that happened almost every time. I would be eating a trail bar and an ant would head for my shoe. As it neared the shoe it would hesitate and turn back. It would go about a foot and turn toward the shoe again. It would reach my shoe and start to climb it. It would hesitate and turn back. It would get off the shoe and walk away a few inches. It would hesitate and turn back. This would be interesting at first and it had my attention because I didn't want to get bitten, but it would get old after a while and I could feel my irritation rising. I would gently pick the ant up in a handful of dirt and toss it five feet away. It would be furious! With great agitation it would travel in circles until it saw my shoe....and head back. I know it takes two to tango. This little dance happened more times than I want to think about.

As I was taking my break I was passed by Freestyle and Body Bag. They stopped for a brief chat. They were super enthusiastic hikers who were fast and in peak condition. The pathway curved through the trees and I passed mountain ponds. There were still small patches of snow next to them and I could only imagine how cold the water was. Shadows of nearby trees and the surrounding granite mountain reflected on the water. Trees had fallen into the ponds and I could see their outlines beneath the water. Freestyle and Body Bag were swimming in one of the ponds. Freestyle said enthusiastically: "The water's great! C'mon in!"

Thanks. But, No Thanks. I continued on. I was still hiking in full, thick, forest near the top of the mountain. I was whistling a song I had been whistling since starting my thru-hike and would continue whistling all the way to Canada. It was an obscure, sad, whiny, little (she done me wrong) song that I can't recollect right now and don't want to. I'm sure if I put on a backpack and headed up a mountain it would pop right back into my mind. I can hum and whistle hundreds of songs. It was frustrating having that song play over and over in head. I whistled tunes a lot during my hike. Two songs I whistled almost every day were "White Christmas" and the "John Dunbar Theme Song" in "Dances With Wolves". "White Christmas" was nostalgic and upbeat. The "John Dunbar Theme Song" was epic, sweeping, and magnificent. Every time I would come upon a magnificent view I would whistle it. I wondered and even worried if I would ever become blasé when beautiful views came into sight. It never happened. There was a break in the trees presenting a fantastic view. I whistled the John Dunbar song.

I was enjoying drinking the iced cold water of the clear mountain streams. I was sweating heavily in the afternoon heat and was staying well hydrated. Maybe too well hydrated. I was pissing about every twenty minutes. This was easy to accomplish. Judge the wind velocity and direction. Turn ninety degrees left or right. Piss. The trick was not having someone catch up to me from either direction while I was doing this. I would stand completely still and listen and watch for motion. It worked. I was never surprised during the entire thru-hike.

In about an hour Freestyle and Body Bag caught up to me. They wanted to talk so they stayed at my speed. We approached a trail that led to the peak of the mountain we were hiking. It was about a quarter of a mile to the top.

Freestyle: "Let's go bag that peak!"

Body Bag: "Yea! Let's Go!"

Jim: I think I'll pass.

They left their packs next to the Trail and headed to the peak. I took out my trail mix, found a shady spot, and watched them climb. By the time they were near the top the small trail had petered out. They were now using handholds and footholds to climb the jagged rocks. It looked dangerous. I didn't want to watch anymore. I continued on. I followed a ridgeline in a treeless area for miles. It wasn't lush with vegetation like the area I hiked in earlier. It was covered with a light brown grass that was tall enough to flow in the wind. There was a pleasant breeze that felt great when it hit my sweat soaked shirt. It felt like evaporative cooling. There were a lot of lizards in this dry area. They were big and black and much larger than the little grey lizards in New Mexico. While taking a break I accidentally invaded a lizard's territory. It was cute watching the little body pumps telling me who was the "boss" around here. It was hot. I was in an exposed area. The sun was beating down relentlessly. Great! Now I have to deal with black flies! From Campo to Canada they were a constant. They were a nuisance. I would watch them buzzing around knowing sooner or later they were going to land. When they did I would feel a tiny gripping on my skin and then the bite. Unlike regular flies they were slow and I would pop them. Ninety percent of the time I would kill them. The trick was to get them when I first felt them grip my skin. I got good at it. I carried a walking stick which freed up one hand. I killed hundreds of black flies. They were persistent and totally focused. If I swatted at one and missed, it would immediately head back for more and I would kill it. Some insects would get the idea. A lot of times I would wave my hand in front of my face to brush away gnats and they would leave. Same with mosquitoes. If I swatted at a mosquito and missed, I could almost see the thought process. "Hey! That was too close! This guy means business! The percentages are not in my favor. I'm outta here!" The black flies never got it. If I missed the first time, there was almost a kamikaze mentality. "You missed! I'll get you this time!" POW!

Pretty soon, Freestyle and Body Bag caught up to me. (Is this sounding like a broken record?) They were high in spirits. Freestyle said: "You are like a metronome, Jim. You steadily move down the Trail." I experienced plenty on my hike and am far from complaining, but do you see how much more young hikers experienced? - and this was just one day. I passed them an hour later as they were taking a break. It was now evening and I started looking for a place to camp. I was on a steep switch backed descent and knew I wasn't going to find anything until I reached the stream at the bottom. I was brushing my hand back and forth in front of my face. Gnats could be a nuisance any time of day. I mainly remember them in the evening. This day was no exception. There were just a few and eventually they left. Other times, though, there could be swarms of them. When that happened I would put on my head net. Freestyle and Body Bag caught up to me and we hiked together. We startled a bear that was fifty feet away and watched it go crashing down the side of the mountain. There was a good camping spot next to the stream. Freestyle and Body Bag were the first to arrive and invited me to join them. There was one big area with a fire pit and a smaller area nearer the stream. Since they had gotten to the campsite first I let them choose the site they preferred. They chose the site with the fire pit and made a big fire. I was glad to get the smaller site next to the stream. The water was flowing rapidly and I was less than ten feet away so it would block any outside noise. I put up my tent. I always found this relaxing. As I was doing this I got into the habit of breathing deeply and slowly and I could feel any tension draining from my body. It was starting to get dark and the temperature cooled quickly. There were mosquitoes that were trying to feast on me. I visited around the campfire for a few minutes and headed to the tent. I hiked twenty-three miles and was pleasantly tired. I knew I would sleep well and did. Once I was inside the tent I would completely empty the backpack. I would inflate the air mattress which was much softer to sit on than the ground. I would take off my shoes and shake out all the dirt. There was always a little pile of dirt at the foot of the tent. I would take off my socks and shake them out. Dust would be floating around the tent for a couple of minutes. I would examine my filthy feet and use the dirty socks to clean them. After 1,648 miles my feet were tough and calloused and I didn't baby them. I changed to my sleeping clothes. It was chilly so I got into my sleeping bag. I took out the trail mix and ate as much as I could. I had a bagel, too. I didn't want to eat anything sugary, like Nutella, pop tarts, or trail bars that could keep me awake. Once I finished eating, I packed the food into the waterproof stuff sack and placed it in a ten gallon plastic trash sack. Anything with a smell went into the sack, too - Purell, suntan lotion, mosquito repellant, toothpaste. I closed and tied the white ten gallon sack, put it into a thick plastic thirty gallon garbage bag, and closed and tied it. The garbage bag went into the bottom of the backpack. I closed the backpack. This wasn't going to be a very cold night so I put my long sleeved shirt into the balaclava and used it as a pillow. I had my four water bottles next to the front entrance and my piss bottle within arm's reach. By this time I was wearing my headlamp. I took out the maps I used during the day, my GPS, and my calendar. This was always a mini-highlight of the day. I would turn on the GPS and it would pinpoint my location on Halfmile's map. I would put a big circle around the location. The GPS gave the miles from Campo - 1,648. The mileage marked on the calendar for the previous day was 1,625. I hiked 23 miles. I always guessed beforehand what the total was going to be. I was usually pretty close. Just before going to sleep, I put the clothes I wore during the day and the wind shirt completely over the closed backpack and tucked them in at the bottom. A bear would have to sniff through a lot of layers to smell my food.

I would lie on my back with my hands behind my head and listen to the night sounds. My breathing would get deeper I would roll onto my side and fall asleep.

It really was an addictive, simple, stress free lifestyle. Day after day, I would get up in the morning, have breakfast, pack up and hike through beautiful forest or desert. I would be listening to birds, trickling streams, and wind whistling through trees. I would see bear, elk, deer, coyotes, marmots, pica, and more commonly, rabbits, squirrels, and chipmunks. I would take breaks every couple of hours, sometimes in areas with jaw dropping views. I would chat with hikers who were having the time of their lives, watch dazzling sunsets, see stars fill the sky and fall asleep in the peaceful quiet of the forest.

The next morning I briefly chatted with Freestyle and Body Bag. They headed out as I was taking down my tent. The destination today was the Seiad Valley Cafe. It was right next to the Trail. It closed at 2:00 pm and I needed to hike fourteen miles to get there. I made it by noon, averaging over three miles an hour. I was motivated. The Seiad Valley Cafe was nominated third on the Travel Channel's "Top Ten Places to Pig Out" in America. It was the home of the Pancake Challenge. The Pancake Challenge was like the Half-Gallon Ice Cream Challenge on the Appalachian Trail. You heard about it long before you got there. It became a much anticipated event. It had been going on for over twenty-five years and only nineteen people had successfully completed it. If a hiker could eat five – inch thick, one pound - pancakes in less than two hours the meal was free. Hikers rooted each other on and when a hiker got close to finishing in the allotted time, he or she would have a cheering audience. Unlike the Half-Gallon Ice Cream Challenge, I actually wanted to take the Pancake Challenge. I wanted to see what kind of dent I could put into five pounds of pancakes. I figured all those carbs would be used to power my way up the Trail and I needed all the calories I could get. Plus, I love pancakes with lots of butter and syrup. I took my place at the counter and asked the waitress about the Challenge. Breakfast ended an hour earlier and it was only for breakfast. Bummer! I was starving, though, and this cafe was ranked third in the top ten places to pig out in America. I didn't stay disappointed for long. I ordered the double cheeseburger with bacon, potato salad, and iced tea. The cheeseburger was huge and delicious. As I was eating, I was sitting next to the blender that was making shakes and malts. The waitress would completely fill the blender with ice cream and turn it on. It was loud but the end result looked delicious. I ordered an Oreo Cookie flavored chocolate malt. I still dream about it.

I started hiking right after lunch. I knew the next eight miles were going to be beyond brutal and was glad to have a good filling lunch under my belt. In the next eight miles there was going to be an altitude gain of 4,500 feet. This area had a reputation for being extremely hot and it was well over 100 degrees. House, Baro, H Bomb, Panama Red, Pit Stop, Body Bag, and Freestyle, all had lunch at the same time I did. They found a shady spot to rest and were going to head out in the late afternoon. As I passed them, Freestyle tactfully asked: "Are you crazy?"

The day was absolutely scorching. To make it even worse, there was a major fire two valleys away. Helicopters were flying overhead with water buckets to douse the blaze. It had been going for over a week and was getting worse. The air was so thick with smoke it was like I was walking in a fog. The climb was a tough one. It was continuously up and relentless. As my lungs strained for air they were taking in large amounts of smoke. I had five quarts of water and was drinking it liberally. Fern Spring was two miles from the start and I was planning to refill my bottles there. When I reached the spring the flow was so slow I could count each drop. Bees had taken over the cool, damp ground and when I put the bottle under the drops they became agitated. That wasn't going to work so I checked my map. The next water was four miles away. I had to start conserving water. It was a good thing I did because the next source was dry. I had two quarts to get to Kangaroo Spring which was six miles away. I planned to spend the night there and it was a reliable water source. I know that sounds like plenty but with the heat and exertion I could have used twice as much. As I neared the top of the mountain I could see the smoke billowing out of the valleys. There were a lot of choppers working the fire and they passed overhead with their water buckets. The fire was heading in the direction of Seiad Valley and I wanted to get out of the area before the Forest Service closed the Trail. They did close the Trail the next day. Whew! Another close call. House had the same idea. He caught up to me at Kangaroo Spring. He cooked his dinner and we chatted. He was even more paranoid and was planning to hike through the night to get out of the area. Freestyle and Body Bag left Seiad Valley in the evening and night hiked. Freestyle told me how the forest fire glowed red in the night and of seeing a tree explode into flames.

Kangaroo Spring was high on the mountain. It was in a big meadow that was enclosed on all sides but one by the surrounding mountain. The meadow was full of long, thick grass and was marshy. I traveled through a lot of mud getting to the spring. It was only about ten feet around and shallow, with slowly flowing water. I could see a lot of animal footprints in the mud next to the spring. This was where animals from miles around came to drink, including Jim. I drank my fill and topped off all of my bottles. The water was cold and good. I camped in a great spot. The wind was from a favorable direction and kept the smoke away. In the night, small animals grazed next to my tent. They were so close they would brush the ropes anchoring the tent. I'm not sure what they were. I could hear the clip clop of their hooves. They weren't a threat and I fell asleep listening to them munching on the grass.

The hiking the next day was miserable. The air was thick with smoke. After a while my lungs ached. It was hard to take a full breath. My eyes were scratchy and bloodshot. I was trying to make it to the Oregon border but ran out of daylight.

My goal for the next day was to make it to Callahan's by dinnertime. Callahan's was a fancy lodge that was hiker friendly. It had an all you can eat spaghetti dinner with a free beer for twelve dollars. For seven dollars you could sleep on the grassy lawn behind the lodge. Breakfast the next morning was bacon, eggs, fresh fruit, and all you can eat pancakes for ten dollars. Callahan's was twenty-nine miles away but to say I was motivated would be an understatement. I wasn't sure when the restaurant closed so I was super motivated! I had spaghetti on my mind!

You hear me talk a lot about food. It became more of a focus as the hike progressed. Thru-hikers had almost no body fat and a metabolism that was through the roof. If we didn't eat enough we would "hit the wall" and have no energy. To recharge our bodies, massive amounts of food were needed. Just like water in the desert, food became an obsession. A lot of times it would be the topic of conversation. While hiking, I would fantasize about the burritos, pastries, and all the good food I was going to eat. My stomach had an attitude problem. When I reached a resupply town it didn't say: "I'm hungry, let's eat." It demanded: "FEED ME! MASSIVELY! NOW!" Three hours after eating I would hear: "I'M HUNGRY! I NEED FOOD!" I would eat a large pizza. Three hours later: "WHAT IS IT ABOUT "FEED ME" THAT YOU DON'T UNDERSTAND?!" It was amazing how much food I and other hikers could consume and it was absolutely necessary to keep us moving down the Trail at peak efficiency.

4 OREGON

I woke up at 5:15 am and the sun was just rising by the time I started hiking. I reached the Oregon border by 7:00 am. There was a register which I signed. It was fun seeing the names of the people I had hiked with. It felt good to have made it all 1,700 miles across California. I took a few minutes to relax, sit down, have some trail mix, and enjoy my accomplishment. Hiking through California had been an amazing adventure. Its variety and sheer beauty far exceeded my expectations. I was smiling as I was reminiscing. I wasn't going to make twenty-nine miles sitting on my butt, though. Back to hiking.

The way other hikers talked about Oregon and the way it was mentioned in guidebooks, I wasn't expecting much. It sounded like a state with not a lot of high mountains where you could concentrate on making big miles. Was I pleasantly surprised! In my opinion Oregon held its own with California and Washington.

In Oregon I spent days hiking through forests with views of nothing but tall fir trees as far as I could see. The mountains were easier right from the start. The Trail was smooth for a change, and heading to Callahan's I hiked full out. I was averaging over three miles an hour which was unusual. Water was plentiful and seasonal streams were flowing. I stopped at Sheep Camp Spring where the cold, clear water was gushing out of a pipe. I even took out my cleaning cloth and had a refreshing body bath. I made it to Callahan's in twelve hours and ten minutes with time to spare before closing. The spaghetti dinner was filling and the beer hit the spot. I was feeling mellow as I listened to the guitarist. The restaurant had an outside dining area that was doing good business. The guitarist was inside and his voice was amplified to the diners outside. He was an excellent singer and guitarist and really added to the dining experience. He had a tip jar and just before I left I put a couple of dollars into it. Right in the middle of his song he stopped, thanked me, and wished me a good hike. It was amplified to the outside diners. It was kind of classy.

There was a big grassy area behind the restaurant to put my tent. I was the first hiker there. Two other hikers joined me a couple of hours later and cowboy camped. As I was putting up my tent I was in full view of the outside diners on an upper terrace. I would look up and see them glancing down at me with curiosity. It was disconcerting. Once inside the tent on the soft grass, I relaxed and listened to a flowing fountain and songs from the guitarist.

I was a wimp only eating two servings of the all you can eat spaghetti the night before. I was determined to make up for it at breakfast and I got my money's worth. The friendly waitress kept the pancakes coming and by the time I finished I was uncomfortably full. The fullness was exactly what I wanted. I knew it would go away in an hour and I would have a lot of calories to burn on my hike. I finished with three excellent cups of coffee with cream and sugar. I gave the waitress a good tip which she deserved.

I had breakfast with Tracks. He was of first or second generation Chinese descent. I heard him speaking fluent Chinese with another hiker. His American accent was flawless and Southern California. He was in his early twenties and had an engaging personality. I leapfrogged with him far into Washington. He was much faster than I was and passed me many times. Each time, he would slow down and we would talk - sometimes for an hour or two. I would pick up my pace so I didn't slow him down too much. I enjoyed his company.

As I was taking down my tent, Early Girl and Water Boy called down to me from the terrace where they were having breakfast and asked if I needed a ride back to the Trail. " You bet!" The Trail was smooth and easy on the feet. The mountains were beautiful and rolling instead of straight up. It was a good day of hiking. The next few days were enjoyable. It was easier to put in long miles and I took advantage of it. I passed a lot of ponds and lakes. Some of the ponds were marshy and stagnant and I needed my mosquito lotion. Some of the lakes were good sized and I passed tourist camping areas. There were resorts next to lakes and many of the hikers would head down to them in search of food. They would pass me on the Trail and in a few hours pass me again and I knew their search had been successful. It was such a temptation when a resort was only two miles from the Trail and there was a double cheeseburger and chocolate malt with my name on it, but for the most part I kept moving. Metronome should have been my trail name.

I ran out of daylight before finding a spot to put my tent. It was overrun with lumpy, thick, grass, but was the best I could find. In the early morning

I heard thunder far in the distance. It seemed to be heading my way. I was in a good area to wait out the storm so I went back to sleep. It never materialized. Tracks caught up to me just before I started hiking. He had been cowboy camped right in the middle of the storm. He was surrounded by thunder and lightning, huge winds, and pelting rain. He was still shaken. I hiked with Tracks off and on for most of the day. By 6:00 pm I made it to Brown Mountain Shelter. It was the only designated shelter on the PCT. The bunks inside were already taken and most of the level camping spots around the shelter were taken, too. The area was full of section hikers congregated around a couple of picnic tables cooking their dinners and deep into conversation. There was well water available and I filled my bottles. As I was doing this I listened to the conversations. These hikers were laughing and joking and groaning and bullshitting and having a great time. There were lots of aching muscles being complained about and blisters being taken care of. There were stories of past exploits and future plans. One guy hiked fifteen miles that day and was letting everyone know of his accomplishment. To be out in the woods was a big deal to these hikers. It was something they had greatly anticipated and now they were doing it. It was fun to see that enthusiasm. Of course, right in the middle of the group, bullshitting with the best of them, was Tracks. That's what I liked about the guy. He was so gregarious he would stop hikers heading in the opposite direction and talk to them. I continued hiking and just before dark found a small smooth spot, surrounded by lava, just big enough for my tent. I hiked twenty-five miles and it hadn't been that difficult.

The next day was spent hiking across lava fields. The area had its own rugged beauty. When flowers would show up they really stood out.

I have no recall of the next day whatsoever. My calendar says I hiked on a lot of lava and hiked twenty-six miles. I looked over Halfmile's maps, what I had written on my calendar, and even Yogi's water report, and couldn't remember anything. I hiked completely alone that day. Tracks was ahead of me and most of the people I was normally around while hiking were partying in Ashland, Oregon. Ashland was a destination for thru-hikers. I noticed while writing about this adventure that I could bring back memories of each day by remembering who I was hiking with on that particular day. The most vivid memories were when I was hiking with or around people whose company I enjoyed. So as much as I talk about enjoying the solitude - and I really did - I enjoyed being part of the hiking community. After seeing the same hikers for hundreds of miles it was fun running into them while hiking. Sometimes we would chat or just a pleasant "Hi" as we passed one another.

My goal for the next day was to get to Mazama Village, which was close to Crater Lake, by early afternoon. I had been putting in big miles since Etna - 23, 24, 26, 29, 22, 25, 19, 26, and was ready for a break. Mazama had a good restaurant, store, showers, and laundry. The store had my resupply box and a letter from Johanna that I was looking forward to. I walked into the little store at 2:00 pm. Just as I was asking for my resupply box, the mailman came in with an envelope from Johanna. It included a much appreciated note and two beautiful cards from Eunie Deter, a friend Johanna walks with. It made my day. Thanks, Eunie. There were picnic tables in front of the store where I sorted through the contents of the resupply box and put them into stuff sacks. I spent the next four hours relaxing, enjoying Johanna's letter, showering, eating 5,000 calories of food, doing laundry, and drinking beer with other hikers. I headed back to the woods in the evening feeling full, happy, and mellow, knowing the next morning I would reach Crater Lake.

I packed up early the next morning and made it to Crater Lake by 8:00 am. What an impressive sight. Crater Lake was created by the collapse of Mt. Mazama after it erupted 7,700 years ago. It created a huge crater that is six miles across. It has no rivers flowing into or out of it. Rain and snow melt keep it at its present level. There are beautiful glaciers on the sides of Crater Lake and it has some of the purest water in North America. What impressed me the most was how blue the water was. To me, it set the standard for what blue should look like. It was perfectly blue. With the tall trees along its edge, steep drop-offs down to the amazingly blue water, and gorgeous reflections, it couldn't have been more impressive. Fortunately, Shack and Weeki arrived just as I took my camera out and I asked another thru-hiker to take our picture. The Trail followed the rim for the next seven miles and I was able to see the blue, blue, sparkling lake from different angles. It was mesmerizing.

I was sorry when the Trail headed away from Crater Lake. There was a lot of lava hiking for much of the day. By evening, I saw Mt. Thielsen for the first time. I had never heard of it before. It was one of the most impressive mountains of all. It was a clear day and the Trail followed a winding pathway near the base of the mountain offering a variety of great views of the glacier covered volcano. I was too lazy to open my pack and take out my camera. I can't believe I didn't take a picture.

I was passing and being passed by Weeki, Shack, and House for most of the day. It was hard finding a camping spot in the evening. We were high on the side of Mt. Thielsen. It was steep and there was a lot of vegetation. House found a tiny spot carved into the mountain about ten feet above the Trail. I kept looking for another half an hour. I had hiked 26.5 miles and could feel it. It was almost dark by the time I found a spot on the upslope next to a giant tree. I pushed around the dirt with my feet to level it. I was so close to the tree that I tied one of the tent ropes onto a branch to secure the tent. Once I had the tent up and was in my sleeping bag I replayed the hike along Crater Lake before going to sleep. The term, happy hiker, would definitely apply.

It was cold starting out the next morning. I was wearing my gloves and three layers of clothing. I was hiking in a lovely area on the side of Mt. Thielsen with views of the volcanic peak on my right and endless views of fir filled forests on my left. There was a bend in the Trail with an overlook just being hit by the first rays of the sun. I took a break, sat down, had some trail mix, and enjoyed the sun warming my body. Shack and Weeki saw me basking in the sun and couldn't resist. They came over and joined me. Shack looked like he was getting his energy back. During the day's hike he easily passed me on high mountain trails. He wasn't even using his hiking stick. Weeki was the one who looked the worse for wear. He was hiking with Cascadia 7 trail runners. He hiked all of California up to Ashland Oregon (about 1,730 miles) on one pair of shoes. In California, I could always tell if Shack and Weeki were ahead of me when I saw Cascadia 7 heel prints with no tread in the front. He now had a new pair of trail runners but was recovering from the damage that was done and as an eighteen year old the recovery was disgustingly quick. I loved watching the interaction between the two of them. Shack was fifty-seven. For the length of their thru-hike which began April 20th and ended on the 5th of October, Shack was pushed many times to his limits. I would see him utterly fatigued. It had to have been hard trying to keep up with a fit, energetic, eighteen year old, but he was. Weeki was well tuned in to his father's endurance. Often they would hike together and there was a genuine camaraderie. Sometimes Weeki would hike ahead, find a shady spot, and wait for his father. Other times, he would hike with hikers nearer his age for a few miles, then find a shady spot to wait for Shack to catch up. Shack gave him plenty of room to interact with other younger hikers and he did. He seemed most happy hiking with Shack. Weeki had an inclusiveness and sense of trust that was given freely - even to an older person like me. I appreciated that. With their New Zealand accents they were an immediate draw. They were popular with other thru-hikers and tourists. They were always having their picture taken by tourists or being given trail magic. Shack had a full white beard and his face showed a lot of character. Weeki's face radiated youthful energy. Shack was obviously very proud of his son. Weeki loved his father and was delighted to share this adventure with him. Their bond grew stronger as their hike progressed. I was fortunate to have hiked with them.

I finished my trail mix and headed off ahead of Shack and Weeki. The Trail was high on the mountain. I could see it far in the distance and watch it head into dense forest. Weeki and Shack passed me and I met up with them again when they stopped at Thielsen Creek. House soon joined us. We discussed the possibility of the Trail being closed in ten more miles due to fire. It was supposed to be contained and in the mop up stage. We had been hearing of this closure for the last week and hoping by the time we got there it would be reopened. A southbound section hiker said it was still closed but he had gone through anyway. We were debating whether to take the closed Trail or the reroute. We didn't come to a conclusion.

We were in an absolutely gorgeous spot. It was a bright, sunny day. A blue, swiftly flowing creek angled its way up the mountain to glaringly white glaciers. We were next to tall, fragrant, ponderosa pines and in a green meadow covered with purple lupine. The rugged peak was outlined against a stunningly blue sky. It was so close I was tempted to climb it. Body Bag and Freestyle probably did.

I was taking a break at the time. Did I summon the energy to spend less than a minute to take my camera out of my backpack and take a picture? Of course not!

I headed out ahead of the rest. I was moving fast and they never caught up to me by the time I reached the yellow tape blocking the Trail. Still closed! Damn! I read the Forest Service message and mulled over whether to take the closed Trail or the reroute. I waited fifteen minutes for Weeki and Shack or House to show up. They didn't. At the bottom of the Forest Service message, in small print, were words that helped me make my decision: "Violations punishable by up to $5,000 fine and/or six months in jail." I felt like a gutless wonder but I didn't want to take the chance.

It was called the Butte Fire and the Forest Service had copies of the reroute. I took a copy and headed out. The reroute headed away from the PCT and added at least another seven miles to the length of the regular Trail. I didn't like that at all!

I was following my twenty-two miles a day average religiously and was ahead of the average by 6.5 miles. Within the first mile I reached Lake Lucille. There was a shady place next to the lake to rest and that is where I met Mother Goose. She was a thick boned, imposing woman in her sixties. Her long grey braids hung down from a cap with the words HIKER TRASH written on the brim. She looked at me sternly: "Have you seen Shack?" "He's behind me, but he might be taking the regular Trail instead of the reroute." "I'm lookin' for him." I was dying to ask but held back. My plan was to limit this conversation and get back to hiking as soon as possible. The hiking for the next couple of hours was pleasant. It was level and smooth with small streams and thick vegetation. I made it to a road with a camping site that had picnic tables and stopped for a break. Mother Goose caught up to me. We looked at the reroute map. The reroute went steeply up the mountain to a small dirt road about a mile away. Mother Goose wanted to skip the designated reroute and road walk all the way to Summit Lake. That would have skipped eight miles of the Pacific Crest Trail. I wanted to take the designated reroute. I wished her luck and headed on my way. It was a steep climb. I had already hiked twenty-eight miles and was feeling it. The sun was setting and it was getting chilly. It was peaceful and quiet as I set up my tent. I was surprised to see Mother Goose show up. She found a spot to put her tent about twenty feet away and we chatted as she went about her camp chores. My normal reaction when people showed up when I had a camping place to myself was: "Damn!" When Mother Goose showed up, I was pleasantly surprised. She was low on water. I had more than enough and let her have a quart. I know she appreciated it. It was a cold night and I was glad to have my twenty degree sleeping bag.

As I got out of my tent the next morning, Mother Goose was already packed and heading out. She had a thermometer and told me the temperature was twenty-eight degrees. It felt like it. I only had shorts and nothing to cover my legs and they were covered with little blue bumps. I should have put on the balaclava but I didn't. When I started hiking, the sun wasn't up and I was freezing. There was a forest road I followed uphill for the next three miles. Three times on my thru-hike I ran into situations where I was too cold. This was one of them. On all three occasions I started hiking as fast as I could. I was hiking uphill at more than four miles an hour. I shot by Mother Goose whose teeth were actually chattering and she kept repeating: "I'm so cold!" As I rapidly hiked uphill I would pass pockets of warmth. The pathway didn't look any different and I couldn't figure out what caused the change, but for a couple of seconds it felt good. Despite the speed it took until the sun came out for my body to warm up. I finally reached the turnoff back into the forest. I needed to head east to get to the Pacific Crest Trail and past the fire reroute. There was a Forest Service sign warning that if you weren't good at navigation to road walk to Summit Lake and catch the Pacific Crest Trail there. I mulled it over and decided to stick with the reroute. It was through dense, mountainous, forest. There was no pathway, but for the first mile there were pink ribbons about every twenty yards. I was thinking this was going to be a piece of cake. I was following the pink ribbons but it was becoming very steep and I was relying heavily on my hiking stick to stay upright. The ribbons ended and I hiked in a wide circle trying to find some semblance of a pathway. There was nothing. I knew I had to head east for the next three miles to rejoin the PCT. I took out my GPS and set it to the nearest waypoint on the PCT. I tried to keep the arrow centered to the waypoint. It sounds easy enough but it wasn't. For the next four miles I was doing a lot of bushwhacking. It was very challenging. I love bushwhacking. I would follow the arrow and it would take me through heavy vegetation, across streams, around bushes, trees, and boulders, and up and down hills. I climbed to the top of a mountain and the arrow pointed directly down the other side. I looked down at sheer drop offs and said "No Way!" I angled around the mountain and for a while tried to visualize the course to the waypoint. When I looked at the GPS a half an hour and a lot of maneuvering later, I was headed in completely the opposite direction. I wouldn't believe it and checked the GPS batteries. Up and down hills, more bushwhacking, a lot of grousing, and I finally reached the waypoint. I made it to Summit Lake by 6:00 pm and was more than ready to call it a day. When I marked my map that night, I could only legitimately account for seven PCT miles. I knew that Shack, Weeki, House, and Mother Goose were far ahead of me. Seven miles had taken me from 6.5 miles over my twenty-two miles a day average, to 8.5 miles in the hole. I was really bummed. It was the lowest point of my hike. I kept thinking about losing ground to Shack, Weeki, House, and Mother Goose and messing up my twenty-two miles a day average. I was brooding and second guessing my judgment: "Maybe I shouldn't have taken the fire reroute. No guts - no glory. Shack, Weeki, and House are a lot bolder than me."

Something wasn't adding up.

I had a very enjoyable day creating a vivid memory of bushwhacking to my heart's content - of pushing through thick underbrush, hopping over logs, climbing rocks, jumping down the other side and landing with a bone jarring "thud", and hiking through areas that probably hadn't seen another human in years. I realized it was time to re-evaluate. I came to the conclusion I was too focused on maintaining the twenty-two miles a day average. It had served me well for nine hundred miles but it was time to end it.

I knew I had the discipline to do ten hours of actual hiking each day. It had become a habit. I knew I had more than enough drive to get to Canada by my goal of the 1st of October. Once I stopped focusing on the twenty-two miles a day I could feel the release of pressure immediately.

The next morning I circled part of Summit Lake. There were lots of campers enjoying the lake. The smell of burning wood and bacon was in the air. An hour into the hike I met Golden Ray. His golden rain cover covered his backpack whether it was raining or not. He was friendly, outgoing, talkative, and deaf. I enjoyed talking with him. A couple of times he handed me a notebook and pencil when he didn't understand what I was saying. Golden Ray was fast. I would see his name in logbooks and notice that he kept getting further ahead of me. He finished over two weeks earlier than I did.

A couple of hours later as I was taking a break, around the corner came U-Haul along with his hiking partners, Tangent and Holstein. That was a shock. I hadn't seen him since Kennedy Meadows at the start of the High Sierras. They stopped and took a break. We caught up on the people we had hiked with. We filled in the gaps. I added a few things he didn't know and he did the same. We talked about the trail magic just before Walker Pass, about Oakie Girl and all the hikers who had been there.

I was glad to hear that all the hikers we met at Oakie Girl's trail magic were still hanging in there. We were enjoying her breakfast burritos on June 15th. At that time we were 650 miles into the hike. We were now in Oregon. It was August 24th. We were 1,900 miles into our hike. It was amazing the details we could recall of that day. I think that was because we spent a lot of time living in the moment, free of distractions. I didn't mention it to U-Haul, but I remembered the dynamics of the group sitting around the table. Bouncer was telling how he got his trail name. It was long and uninteresting and seemed to go on forever. His delivery was good, though, and everyone was laughing at the right places. This was the first time I had seen Bouncer and Scalawag. They dominated the conversation. Typo (Jeremy) from New Zealand was spending most of his time typing on his computer and looking up and laughing when everyone else laughed. Kieshi was on his second beer and mellow and planning to spend the night. There was bad chemistry between Shawn Murphy, who wasn't afraid to express his opinion, and Scalawag and Bouncer. They would take little jabs at Shawn. He seemed to enjoy it and gave it right back.

U-Haul was glad to be out of the hot sun and was contributing to the conversation but not trying to dominate. Oakie Girl knew she had a live group and was sitting back and enjoying it. Jim was happily stuffing his face with food.

I passed ponds, meadows, and hiked through thick, healthy forest for most of the day. I was taking another break when David and Brit caught up. I hadn't seen them in a long time. The turnoff to Shelter Cove Resort was less than a mile away and they were heading to the restaurant. We got caught up on people we had hiked with. I was curious about Magic Bag but they hadn't heard anything about him.

They headed down the Trail and that was the last I saw of them. By the time they reached Washington they were hiking thirty plus mile days.

I camped beside lakes the next three days and loved it. I passed Lower Rosary Lake which had a designated campground that was full of hikers. Middle Rosary Lake was smaller and hikers were tented in a smooth, inviting area. I ended the day at North Rosary Lake. What a great spot! It was much smaller and more primitive than the other two lakes. I couldn't see any area that had been used to put a tent. I made my own spot. When I left the next morning I made it look like no one had been there. I was tented twenty feet from the lake. There was a downed tree only five feet from the water. Between the tree and the water was a sandy beach. I sat down, leaned my back against the tree, and had my dinner. The sun was setting and its rays were hitting the water causing it to glitter. Water bugs darted across the top of the water. A fish zapped one and splashed back into the water causing a ripple that came all the way to my feet.

As I write about my Pacific Crest Trail hike, some of the memories that bring back the best feelings are the places I camped. By the end of the day I was glad to be finished and could relax and unwind. I rarely felt endorphins while I was hiking but they kicked in at the end of the day and created "life is good and I'm lucky to be out here" feelings.

Mother Goose passed as I was taking down my tent. I caught up to her an hour later and spent some time hiking and talking with her. She was an interesting lady. She had a no nonsense personality that was almost gruff. She told me she tried to hike two thousand miles each year. She was trying to make it to Canada and if she made it she would have hiked 36,000 miles. Say that again, please? "36,000 miles." WOW! It was mind boggling. I have forgotten how many times she said she hiked the Appalachian Trail but it was a lot. She was the first woman to yo-yo the Appalachian Trail. (Hike from Springer Mountain, Georgia to Mt. Katahdin and turn around and hike back to Springer Mountain.) She had hiked all the sections of the Pacific Crest Trail. Some of them she had hiked many times. The section of Oregon that we were hiking was one of her favorites and she provided a wealth of information. Her goal is to hike 50,000 miles by age 80. I wouldn't bet against her.

The mountains in Oregon were beautiful. There were green, healthy forests and meadows full of blue and sometimes purple lupine. If you haven't smelled lupine it has a fresh delicate smell that will stop you in your tracks and make you inhale and exhale like a bellows.

There was a small tranquil lake that called to me. I stopped at 5:00 pm which was a good two hours earlier than normal. In my mind I was making a statement that I wasn't going to be a slave to the twenty-two miles a day average. It felt good to casually go about my camp chores and enjoy the tranquility of my surroundings. I slept well that night.

The next morning, mist was swirling slowly over the lake and my tent was covered with condensation, both inside and out. I packed up a wet tent and could feel the extra weight. Mother Goose passed me as I was taking down my tent. When I caught up to her I complained about the condensation, the wet tent, and the extra weight. I didn't get the sympathy I was hoping for but did get some good advice. Around lakes and ponds she said to put my tent under big, thick, trees. I took her advice when I camped next to Sisters Lake that night. The next morning mist over the lake was so thick it was almost a fog. I could see animal tracks on the dew saturated ground. My tent was dry.

I hiked by mountain lakes with their blue water shimmering in the morning sun. I passed grass filled colorful alpine meadows full of red, orange, blue, purple, yellow, and white flowers. By early afternoon, clouds started to cover the sky and the wind began to pick up. It was getting cold. Thunder rumbled and the sky darkened. I passed meadows where hikers were sitting next to campfires. I could smell the smoke, hear the crackling fires, see sparks flying up, and imagine the warmth.

There were imposing volcanoes in the distance. For miles, I hiked up and down lava fields getting closer to the volcanoes. I passed isolated trees that were dead. All that was left were their eerily white skeletons shining against the dark red lava and dark sky. Low, dark, clouds now filled the sky and were moving rapidly. Thunder continued to rumble creating a dark brooding atmosphere. On ridges I was being battered by the wind and having a hard time staying on the pathway. I knew what the lava was doing to my shoes and could imagine what it would do to my skin if I fell. I hiked twenty-three difficult miles before stopping a mile short of the highway leading to Sisters, Oregon. My feet were throbbing. It was windy and cold during the night and my legs were cold. I only had shorts and realized I needed more. That became a priority when I reached Sisters.

I was lucky early the next morning when I hitchhiked from McKenzie Pass to Sisters, Oregon. I waited about fifteen minutes before the first car came winding up the little mountain road. A couple in their mid-fifties stopped for me. They had just finished a week long hike and were heading home. They couldn't have been more enthusiastic about backpacking and asked a lot of questions. When we reached Sisters they still weren't finished with their questions and invited me for a latte and scone. They knew all about Sisters and told me the places to visit. They even took my picture and sent it to my computer. The latte and scone were excellent, but just an appetizer, and I headed for a real breakfast. I didn't plan to spend the night in Sisters but planned to spend a leisurely day resupplying. Sisters, Oregon had a good feel to it. It was a tourist town and thru-hikers weren't a priority but the people I met went out of their way to be helpful and friendly. I had a pounds worth of Halfmile's maps I wanted to send home. I walked to the Post Office. There was a hiker box at the Post Office with three pounds of good tasting granola and I added it to my pack. That was the first time I used food from a hiker box. I had looked at food in hiker boxes from the beginning and nothing looked appetizing. Hikers were getting tired of the good food they packed into their resupply boxes months earlier. From Sisters on, I continued using food from hiker boxes. I next went to an ATM and took out $200. That was the amount I always took out when I needed it. The laundry was nearby and I headed there. Weeki was doing his laundry and we chatted. Shack and Weeki were a full day ahead of me. When they left town they would be hitchhiking to Santiam Pass which was twenty miles further down the Trail. He told me they made it all the way to the end of the fire area without seeing a firefighter but right at the entrance they saw some fire officials. They weren't sure what to do so they hid in the bushes. House walked by and waved to the officials who cheerfully waved back. Shack and Weeki left their hiding place and nonchalantly gave the fire officials a nice wave as they walked by.

After laundry, I headed to a great Mexican Restaurant for a huge chicken and bean burrito. I headed to the grocery store to resupply. Next to the grocery was a Goodwill Store and I found some Nike running pants for $3. I wore them each night for the rest of the hike. They added extra warmth and made a big difference. The grocery store was owned by the employees who were super friendly and helpful. The prices were fantastic and they had everything hikers needed. I couldn't help myself and bought about five extra pounds of food. I could really feel it heading back to McKenzie Pass.

When I reached McKenzie Pass it was almost 7:00 pm and there were good camping spots nearby. I leisurely set up my tent, had dinner, and was in my sleeping bag by 8:00 pm. It wasn't even dark so I lay in my sleeping bag and mapped out my hiking strategy for the next few days. I hadn't had a day off since leaving the Pryor's and my body and mind were starting to feel that little "fog" of fatigue I felt in the Sierras. I had way too much food in my pack so I decided to eat as much as I could every time I took a break. I decided to sleep in each morning as long as I wanted. This was going to be a hiking vacation. I wasn't going to worry about the miles. Just before going to sleep I heard a couple of hikers set up their tent about fifty feet from mine. They were quiet and by 9:00 pm I was sound asleep. I slept until 7:00 the next morning.

I unzipped my tent and looked out and there were Nate and Jenna getting ready to head out. It was a pleasure to see them again. We talked. It was obvious they were still having a great time. It was a good start to the day and I needed a good start. My feet still hadn't recovered from all the lava hiking and the day began with miles more of the torturous stuff. In no time the sun was radiating off of the hot lava and I was drenched in sweat. I finally cleared the lava fields and headed into the forest.

I knew I was approaching the 2,000 mile point and had my GPS out, counting down the miles. Unlike the midway point, the 2,000 mile point was a big deal to me. I kept repeating: "Two thousand miles. That's a lot of hiking. Only 660 miles to go. I can do this." When I reached the 2,000 mile mark there were shady trees with a flat, smooth, area to sit. Someone had formed the number 2,000 in pinecones. Jenna put fresh ferns around the pinecones which was a nice touch. I ate a bag of chocolate chip cookies to celebrate. There must have been thirty of the little cookies in the bag.

By 7:00 pm I was nearing Santiam Pass and started looking for a place to put my tent. Nothing looked good so I crossed the busy highway at Santiam Pass and headed up into the mountains. I hiked through a burn area, over more lava, and ended the day high on a ridge. I was putting up the tent in the dark when I was passed by a family of day hikers heading down to the pass. It didn't look like they even had a flashlight. The father and mother had a strong accent from India. The fourteen year old daughter and twelve year old son had no accent whatsoever. The daughter was model gorgeous: "Hey, lookit' the full moon, Mom."

"Yes. It is bu-ti-ful."

I realized they knew exactly what they were doing. The full moon lit up the pathway and reflected off of the branches of the burned trees giving them a soft white glow. It was bu-ti-ful.

A couple of deer grazed near my camping spot in the early morning and bounded over the ridge when I opened my tent. I hiked in the shade of trees for a few miles. There were little lakes that made great spots to take a break. I passed right at the base of Three Fingered Jack and more lava hopping. I hiked for a time with Nate and Jenna. They were trying to make it to Timberline Lodge by Labor Day (September 3rd) and were planning thirty mile days to get there. I camped next to a lake that night and chatted with them before they headed out to make more miles. That was the last time I saw them. I missed them by hours when I reached White Pass in Washington but with their youth they pulled ahead of me. When I finished my hike and was back home I checked out their journal on PCT-L. It is an excellent journal. They finished on September 29th.

Timberline Lodge was a destination all thru-hikers looked forward to. It was right at the base of the gorgeous, glacier covered Mt. Hood. They were celebrating their 75th anniversary on Labor Day and had a lot of events planned. Thru-hikers were trying to make it there by Labor Day. It was built in the 1930's by the WPA. I remember seeing it for the first time on a television program that featured National Forest Service lodges. It was impressive. It was made of stone. There was a massive stone fireplace directly in front of you as you entered. The high ceiling was supported by thick wooden beams. It was primarily a ski lodge but was popular year round and had a fine restaurant that catered to the wealthy. Most rooms were in the $200+ range. It had an all you can eat breakfast and lunch buffet that was the talk of the Trail.

I was eating massive amounts during breaks and not pushing the pace. I wasn't about to do thirty mile days. I caught up to Mother Goose the next morning. I was surprised to see her. She must have skipped Sisters, Oregon. Mother Goose lived for hiking. She had a knowledge of the area that was amazing. I only asked her a navigation question once and got such a detailed answer I never asked again. She knew the names of every trail junction and side trail out there. She also knew where the problem areas were and filled me in on those whenever we approached one. She talked about an upcoming snowpack covering a rapidly flowing stream. Unlike California that had a low snow year, Oregon and Washington had a heavy snow year. When I crossed the snowpack later in the day it was so thick it looked like a glacier. It was over thirty feet wide. The water was supplied by a nearby glacier and was gushing. There were well defined tracks over the snowpack but the sound of the gushing water directly beneath my feet made my skin crawl. When I made it across there was a three foot gap between the snow pack and the stream bank. I looked down at the gushing water. Other hikers had hopped that gap and I did too, but with trepidation.

Mt. Jefferson was in the distance. It was imposing and impressive. I even managed to take two pictures of it. This was Saturday, September 1st, two days before Labor Day. The area around Mt. Jefferson was filled with hikers enjoying the holiday. I was stopped by hikers wanting to talk to a thru-hiker. Anything I said elicited ooohs and aaahs. It was kind of fun. There was a fire restriction area for the next eleven miles. It was already afternoon and I was on a hiking vacation. I found a spot near a large lake and staked it out. It was near blueberry bushes and I spent a half an hour leisurely picking and eating warm, juicy blueberries.

The hiking the next day was truly spectacular. I started off hiking through meadows and valleys surrounded by glacier covered mountains. I took a break next to a glacier. The ground was covered with an emerald green moss and tiny delicate violets. I filled my water bottle from the dripping glacier. The water was iced cold and delicious.

There was a steady climb to a ridge. Once I reached the ridge the views were vast and awesome. The Trail headed steeply down over a glacier for the next five hundred yards. I would have glissaded if I had known how. With my inexperience the descent had my heart pumping. I zigzagged down, heavily depending on my hiking stick for support. There were jagged rocks at the bottom. I took my time. If I had started sliding I don't know if I would have just picked up speed or been able to break my fall. I was relieved when I made it to the bottom. I was above tree line looking down on lakes and mountains far in the distance. I was on a gradual descent in this wide open area and thoroughly enjoying it. I caught up to Mother Goose and found out she was planning to get to Timberline Lodge for the breakfast buffet on September 5th. That was my plan, too.

I reached Ollalie Lake Resort which was only a quarter mile from the Trail by 5:00 pm. I had a couple of Pepsi's and three huge chocolate chip cookies and met Bowleg. He was in his early twenties and one of the few hikers who preferred to hike alone. There was an instant bond. I found a spot to put my tent at 8:00 pm. I had only hiked nineteen miles. The lower mileage and eating extra food was working. I could feel my energy returning.

I woke up the next morning recharged and ready to go. The hiking was not difficult so I went full out. I passed a couple of big lakes overflowing with weekend warriors. I hiked thirty-two miles. Just as it was getting dark I passed Bowleg as he was taking a break. I had last seen him at the Ollalie Lake store at 6:00 pm the previous day. It was now 7:00 pm. We had hiked thirty-seven miles. I was starting to look for a place to put my tent. He was planning a night hike to reach Timberline Lodge by breakfast the next morning. When did the guy sleep?

After a thirty-two mile day I realized I was going to make it to Timberline Lodge a day early. I just needed to hike fifteen miles to get there. I planned a leisurely pace that would get me there by 3:00 pm. The hiking was easy and there were beautiful views of Mt. Hood. The skies were smoke free and blue.

I reached Wapinitia Pass in the morning and there was a hiker register just before the road. It had the names of almost every hiker that had come through the pass and the date they came through. I noticed there was only one thru-hiker ahead of Mouse. By the time he reached Wapinitia Pass on July 13th I was 1,079 miles behind, visiting the Pryor's. Iron was making good time, too. It was interesting to see where I was in relation to other thru-hikers I had hiked with. I was delighted to see Magic Bag's name on the register. He was a day ahead of me. I was sorry to have missed him. He night hiked a lot and probably passed me in the night. I never did see him again. I know he started putting in big miles and hiked with Brit and David through most of Washington.

I made it to Timberline Lodge by 3:00 pm. The last three miles were steeply uphill through loose sand that had my legs burning. My timing was lousy. I didn't want to spend the night at the lodge but I was dying to have the all you can eat breakfast. I went to the front desk. They were having a thru-hiker special - seventy-five dollars for a room. The room had a bunk bed, small table, a couple of chairs, and a wash basin. There was a communal toilet and shower down the hall. The walls were paper thin. I could hear a whisper in the next room. I took a shower and headed to dinner. There was a big fancy dining room. I looked at the menu and gasped. I could resupply for a week for what they were charging for a dinner without a beverage or dessert. I headed to the bar and grill hoping for a hamburger. There was one waiter. He had fifteen people he was taking care of. I sat for five minutes before I was given a menu and a glass of water. I looked at the prices. Yikes! No hamburgers, but there was a Panini for $18. I was hungry and decided to order it. The waiter was determined not to make eye contact or even acknowledge me. I'm spending $18 for a lousy Panini and getting this kind of service? Forget it! I headed back to my room. I was really hungry but settled for trail mix.

I was the first person in line for breakfast the next morning. Since I was a guest at the lodge I had a ticket for a $4 discount in my hot little hand. I was bubbling with anticipation.

When we lived in Fort Worth, Texas, Johanna and I were heavily involved in tennis. There was an upcoming tournament. Johanna was entered in the 16 and under age bracket and I was entered in the 12 and under. I was ten years old.

The Van Zandt's invited all participants in the tournament to their home for a party. Their son was in the tournament. They lived in a mansion whose back yard sloped down to the fairway of the Colonial Country Club. If you are a golf fan you have heard of the Colonial Country Club. Dad, Mom, Johanna, Doug, and I had on our best clothes. As we arrived, Mr. and Mrs. Van Zandt greeted us at the door.

Mrs. Van Zandt was in her late thirties and radiated style and high society. Think Jacqueline Kennedy.

Pretty soon, Johanna found friends to talk with and Doug was young enough to tag along with Mom and Dad. I was left on my own. I wandered around checking things out and came to a huge crystal bowl that stopped me in my tracks.

Remember in the old Loonie Tune Cartoons when one of the cartoon characters would see a beautiful female and his eyes would spring out of their sockets? When I saw what was in that bowl, my eyes went SPROING! The punch bowl was filled all the way to the top with M&M's. Thousands of them! As a family we never wanted for anything but Dad and Mom lived well within their means. To give you an example, Coca Cola used to have a six ounce bottle. Johanna and I would split the bottle. We thought everyone did. So when I saw this incredible amount of my favorite candy in the whole wide world, I had to act! I grabbed a handful of M&M's and stuffed them into my mouth. Aahhh! Heaven on Earth! I grabbed a handful in my left hand and a handful in my right hand. Dad picked this moment to walk by the punchbowl. Mrs. Van Zandt did, too. She smiled. Dad was horrified: "JIM! YOU KNOW BETTER THAN THAT!" All I could say was "mmmfffttt". Mrs. Van Zandt could see the humor in the situation. Her kind eyes twinkled and she laughed. "That's quite all right. That's what they are there for." There was thunder and disappointment in Dad's eyes.

Heading back to the present: I am the first person in line for the all you can eat breakfast. The waiter signals me that the buffet is open. I follow him to my table.

I am looking over his shoulder at the mouthwatering display of food. I head to the buffet table. There is batter for a do it yourself waffle iron. The waffle is hot, crisp, and golden. There is warm maple syrup and an amazing assortment of fruit toppings. I choose fresh blueberries. I add chocolate chip sprinkles. I look around. I have never seen such a variety of breakfast food. I am first in line. It couldn't be any fresher. I have the hiker hunger. I fill two large plates. The plates are finished in no time. Delicious!

Just like the bounty of M&M's, there is a bounty of incredibly delicious food! I can't stop myself! I go back for seconds, thirds, and fourths, always heaping my plates completely full. The waiter keeps strong, hot, coffee coming. By the fourth trip I am running out of gas. My plates are heaped full of food and I barely manage to finish them. Just as I am leaving,

Mother Goose shows up and I visit with her for a few minutes. I'm a happy hiker. The all you can eat breakfast at the Timberline Lodge has more than lived up to its reputation.

I head back to my room knowing I have really overdone it. Checkout time is 11:00 am. I don't want to do anything but plop down on the bed and try to digest the massive amount of food. Check out time comes too soon and I head back to the Trail. That has to have been the most calories I have eaten, at one time, in my life. It truly was wonderful food and an ecstasy of eating!

Back on the Trail I was still feeling bloated and lethargic. That feeling lasted another hour and then all the food energy kicked in. The hiking was absolutely gorgeous. I spent hours hiking around the base of Mt. Hood. It was covered with huge glaciers glistening in the sun. The glaciers created streams and rivers whose swiftly flowing water churned up dirt and sand and made the water silty. I definitely passed on drinking it. There were many deep, narrow, canyons. As I was nearing a canyon I watched the far side of the canyon wall collapse. I heard the rumble and felt the vibrations about the same time as a huge column of dust rose from the canyon floor. I was glad to see the Trail head away from the side of the canyon. I came to a stream crossing where the water was moving so rapidly I didn't want to mess with it. Fortunately, two pine trees had fallen across the stream on top of one another. They were about eight feet over the water. I held onto one of the trees as I maneuvered on top of the other. It was awkward, challenging, and fun. Once I made it to the far side I was still over the raging water and had to climb over the tangled roots of the downed tree. It had my total attention.

Later in the day I took a one mile side trail to Ramona Falls. The trail headed down into a small canyon, thick with old, shady, trees. The falls were at least thirty feet wide and dropped one hundred feet over a basalt cliff. As the water bounced off of the black rock it seemed to glow. It was a hot day. It felt good taking a break under the shady trees next to the cool, cascading water.

I saw Mt. St. Helens, Mt. Adams, and Mt. Rainier while I was hiking high on a mountain the next day. They were slightly obscured by smoke from fires but were still magnificent. Mt. St. Helens was the volcano I most looked forward to seeing. I could see its wide, jagged top created by a violent eruption in 1980.

I remember watching the drama of that event as it played out on TV and seeing the absolute devastation it created. There was an old hermit who lived in the danger zone who adamantly refused to leave his home. I remember listening to him being interviewed knowing he would soon be dead. After the eruption he was obliterated. That left a lasting impression.

My watchband was on its last legs and the rotted leather that held it to the watch finally gave way. I caught the watch as it was sliding off of my wrist. I knew I would be in Cascade Locks, Oregon in a couple of days so I put the watch into my pocket.

My goal for the next day was to take the Eagle Creek alternate trail and reach Tunnel Falls before dark. The Eagle Creek alternate route was 15.4 miles and bypassed the regular PCT. Almost every thru-hiker took it. It was supposed to be spectacular. I was having a low energy day and the hiking was difficult. By the time I reached the Indian Springs Trail that descended to the Eagle Creek Trail, I was in a foul mood. The trail was overgrown and very steep in places. There were times where my shoes were sliding down the dirt pathway and I was almost out of control. I was muttering to myself that with this much effort this better be good.

After a mile I made it to the Eagle Creek Trail. The Trail was wide and well maintained. I headed through a healthy forest into a deep, narrow, canyon. Far below was Eagle Creek. I hiked along the side of the canyon on a pathway that, at times, was cut into the tall, vertical, basalt cliffs. As I approached Tunnel Falls the pathway narrowed and became wet and slippery. There were sheer, steep drop-offs. Moss was growing on the rock walls and was saturated with water which dripped onto the trail. There was a cable line attached to the rock wall that I gratefully grabbed onto. I was in a narrow, thirty foot wide gorge. A massive amount of water was shooting over the falls. It dropped one hundred and thirty feet before crashing into the basin. The sound was amplified by the narrowness of the gorge and was jarring. A tunnel was blasted into the rock behind the waterfall in 1910. Standing beside the tunnel and being hit by the overspray, I could feel the raw power of the thundering water.

I thought Tunnel Falls would be the highlight but it just kept getting better. The gorge remained narrow and the walls high and vertical for another mile. I passed beautiful waterfalls. This area had a lot of rain each year and had the feel of a humid, tropical rain forest. Some of the trees were completely covered with moss. Ferns and moss covered most of the ground. The dirt was black, fertile, and had a pungent smell. It was so different from any area I had hiked through, it seemed magical. By now it was almost dark and I needed to find a spot to put my tent. The trail headed down to Eagle Creek and I found a great place to camp right next to the water. The sound of the rapidly flowing water put me to sleep in no time.

The next morning I hiked four more miles through this magical area. I came to Punch Bowl Falls. Eagle Creek narrowed into a channel only five feet wide. As the speed of the water increased, it looked like a ladle as it shot out and dropped far down to a basin shaped like a punchbowl. There was a shady spot high above Punchbowl Falls where I stopped for a break under moss covered trees.

The Eagle Creek Trail was popular. I saw a lot of hikers with daypacks as I made my way to the trailhead. Once I reached the trailhead I followed a bike path for the next three miles to the little town of Cascade Locks. The bike path was closed to cars and was an old highway built in the early 1920's. It had a lot of character. It was beautifully maintained. There were small placards telling the history of the old road. On the placards were pictures of people from the 1920's, in their cars, waving to the camera. There was a small stone bridge with a rest stop next to it. In front of the rest area was a plaque showing a family having a picnic next to their old Model T Ford. Nothing had changed. The bridge and the rest area were exactly the same. I could visualize that family having their picnic right in front of me. The old road wound through the shady forest. It was a great approach into Cascade Locks.

I liked Cascade Locks. It was a little tourist town overlooking the Columbia River Gorge. The locals had a short window to make money from the tourists and that was where they focused. I liked Cascade Locks because of the thru-hikers. It was an upbeat atmosphere. We were about to enter Washington - the last state on our journey. There was a feeling we had made it this far and were going to make it all the way. I was ready for a good motel break and planned to spend the next twenty-four hours eating, relaxing, and sleeping.

I also needed to figure out a plan for finishing this thru-hike. Unlike the young hikers who seemed to be hitting their peak, my sixty-five year old body was starting to feel the effects of hiking 2,155 miles. As the miles were getting easier for the younger hikers, I was working harder to maintain my mileage. My body was still in pretty good shape. There weren't any problem areas but there were times I felt fatigued. It was now the 7th of September. I jotted on my calendar: "The days are getting shorter. It's dark by 7:15 pm and light enough to hike at 6:30 am." So far the weather had been on my side but I couldn't depend on it. The mountains in Washington were higher and more challenging than in Oregon and the hiking would be more difficult all the way to the end. I groaned at the thought, but with less time in the day to hike and still needing the high mileage, I had to start asking more of my body to make it to Canada before the snows. A couple of times the previous week I had upped my steady pace and pushed hard for most of the day. It left me tired but not exhausted. I decided to increase my pace on the up hills and level areas and listen closely to my body. I was still sleeping well and decided to try for nine hours of sleep each night to help recharge my body. I grumbled that in twenty-three miles I would have hiked the distance of the Appalachian Trail and I still had the whole state of Washington to hike – 500 Freaking Miles!

I checked in at the Columbia Gorge Inn at 11:00 am. It was a quiet little motel. I was given a clean, spacious, room with a king sized bed. It felt great to take a shower, feel clean, then plop down on a comfortable bed and take a long nap.

I called Doug and sobbed on his shoulder. Poor, tired, Jim. He was patient, sympathetic, understanding, and his enthusiasm for my hike cheered me up.

Thank you, Doug.

I called my next door neighbor, Joyce, who was staying at my house and taking care of Fred. Joyce and Fred have a special bond and I knew he couldn't be in better hands. I had nine resupply boxes lined side by side in my bedroom with the name and address of each of the little mountain towns they would be sent to. I had an envelope next to each one with the postage. I would give Joyce a call a few days before reaching one of the towns and she would drive to the Post Office and mail the resupply box. My resupply box was always there when I reached town. I ran into many thru-hikers having to wait a day or more for their resupply box to show up and they were Pissed! Thank you, Joyce. Great job!

I hit nearly every restaurant in town. I stopped at a burger place that had a list of over thirty milk shakes to choose from. I ordered the peanut butter shake then changed my mind and decided on a chocolate shake. The person making the shake had already added peanut butter and asked if I would like to add chocolate to it. I did. I can highly recommend a chocolate/peanut butter milk shake. There was a grocery store that knew what thru-hikers needed. I loaded up with lots of good food. The little store didn't have a watchband so I had to improvise. Back in the motel room I cut the elastic waistband out of the Nike pants that I slept in. The pants were still snug. I cut the waistband to the right length and tied it onto both sides of the watch. There were little knots on both ends and the elastic was only half the width of the regular watchband. A lot of the metal was showing and it looked pretty tacky. If there was such a thing as climbing the ladder of thru-hiker trashdom, I felt my watchband was giving me a step up. I was still wearing it when I returned home. After fixing the watch, I took another nap, watched some TV, and called it a night. I had a deep restful sleep which was just what my body needed.

I had a huge breakfast the next morning, went back to my room, and slept until 11:00 am. Before leaving town I had two 900 calorie burritos and a coke. By the time I left Cascade Locks, I felt great.

5 WASHINGTON

I crossed the Columbia River on The Bridge Of The Gods and entered Washington - the third and final state. It was a spectacular old steel girder bridge that was over half a mile long. It looked like it had been constructed by a gigantic erector set. It was high enough over the water that ships could easily pass underneath. It had no walkway. The narrow two lane road was a thick steel mesh and as I was walking, I was looking straight down over my toes to the water far below. A breeze was coming up from the water and billowing my shorts. Cars and trucks were passing from both directions and I had to stop and hug the railing at times. A barge about a mile away was heading toward the bridge. It looked like it would get to the bridge while I was directly over it. The timing was perfect. I could see the pilot steering the barge. I was tempted to spit just for the hell of it, but refrained. From the bridge there was a view over the Columbia River Gorge to high mountains far in the distance. There was a mountain with massive cliffs at the top. I looked at it and groaned, having little doubt I would be right next to those cliffs in a few hours.

An hour into the climb I caught up to Mother Goose. How many times have you heard me use that phrase? I was always catching up to Mother Goose. She hiked at a steady two miles an hour, didn't take a lot of breaks, started earlier each morning than I did, and finished just before dark. After 35,500 miles of hiking she had a very efficient system for making miles. I was always startled to see her. I knew I was hiking faster than she was. I realized she was giving me some of my own medicine. Other thru-hikers were probably thinking the same thing about me: "I've been zooming by this guy for over 1,000 miles. He's slow. What goes, here?" Looking back, other than when I passed David and Brit which was more of a game, the

112

only time I passed a thru-hiker who was not taking a break or limping with injury and was actually hiking, was at mile 240 in the California desert. I wasn't slow but I was very steady. I was still catching up to thru-hikers I had never seen before. Most of the hikers I was around started in April. Very few started in May.

I enjoyed catching up to and chatting with Mother Goose. I think we were kindred spirits. We were the same age. We both loved to walk and loved the outdoors. On a number of occasions I swore this would be my last long distance hike. Mother Goose would nod patiently but I could see in her eyes she wasn't buying it. I was sorry to see that she was having a problem with her knee. She was taking heavy doses of a prescribed pain killer and it didn't seem to be working. She was using her hiking poles more like crutches.

As we were walking along, Mother Goose said: "Look at all the blackberries."

"Huh?"

"The blackberries! Don't you see them? They're all over the place!"

"Really?"

She was showing signs of frustration: "Right here! Look!"

"Oh Yea"

I may have been sensitive, but I think I heard a little snort of derision. ......I hope Doug's wife, Ingrid, and daughters, Aurora and Karin, who have an eye for finding edible berries, aren't doing the same as they read this.......

Mother Goose also pointed out huckleberries. I passed fields of them in Oregon and didn't know it. Washington was full of huckleberry bushes and I ate my share. There were lots of blueberries in Washington, too.

The Trail headed steadily up and I leapfrogged the rest of the day with Spatula, Mismatch, and Pitstop. I actually talked with Pitstop. Since Northern California we had passed one another and glared at each other in passing. I'm not sure why. I don't remember who initiated the conversation but he turned out to be an interesting, enthusiastic hiker. I finally made it to the top of the mountain. There was a view of glacier covered Mt. Rainier. When Pitstop, Mismatch, and Spatula caught up, they stopped for a break. I asked Pitstop to take my picture. I told about my disposable camera with the twenty-seven shots. They were amazed. Pitstop said he had already taken over 1,200 pictures. We talked about where I should stand and I could sense that Pitstop was getting nervous. "Twenty-seven pictures. This is a lot of pressure. I hope I don't choke." Finally I was ready and I smiled a toothy smile for the camera ...and smiled....and smiled.... The toothy smile faded into a befuddled look and he snapped the picture.

When I reached the cliffs I had seen from the bridge, I looked out over the Columbia River Gorge. There were ships, barges, tugboats, excursion boats and motor boats busily going about their business. I could see the tiny dot that was my motel. I started heading down from the top of the mountain. It was evening and dark clouds were forming. I could hear thunder in the distance. I found a good place to put my tent down in the trees. Around 10:00 pm a thunderstorm came through. Right in the middle of the thunderstorm I heard Mismatch, Pitstop, and Spatula heading rapidly down the Trail. It rained steadily through the night and the ground was saturated the next morning. The forest smelled wonderful. I was camped on pine needles and I inhaled their piney fragrance as I took down the tent. For most of the day I was high on the mountain, hiking through a forest thick with dripping vegetation. It was cold. I was wearing everything I owned and just barely warm enough. It stayed cold all day. I even saw tiny snowflakes that lasted a few minutes.

In Washington right from day one the forest changed and stayed that way to the end. Washington gets a lot of rain each year. We were warned it could rain nearly every day. All the rain created a green, dense forest full of shady trees, plants and thick vegetation. Almost immediately I started seeing more animals. There were more birds in the trees, squirrels, chipmunks, marmots, and picas. I saw three elk, a number of deer, and a bear in the first three days.

This was bow hunting season. I passed hunters in their camouflage clothes carrying compound bows and heading to the hunt. "Hey. You seen any elk?" "Nope. Sure haven't." I startled a big buck that took off within a minute of hunters heading my way. I wasn't about to tell them what I had seen. I was rooting for the deer.

I was taking a break eating some trail mix when a hunter stopped to chat. He was a good conversationalist, i.e., bull shitter, and after a while he sat down and made himself right at home. He had a blind in a tree a couple of hundred yards away and had seen a mother bear and two cubs walk underneath the tree earlier in the day. He was eager to talk about mountain lions. I think he had this discussion with a lot of hikers. On the Appalachian Trail the fear of thru-hikers was bears. On the Continental Divide Trail the fear has got to be grizzlies. On the Pacific Crest Trail mountain lions almost always entered the conversation. I never talked to a thru-hiker who had an actual encounter with a mountain lion but damn near every thru-hiker knew another hiker, or an uncle, or someone who had an encounter. The thru-hikers who told the mountain lion stories the most convincingly and most often were the ones who hiked far into the night to catch up to and camp with their buddies. In their stories, their friend was awakened by a sound in the night. He turned on his headlamp. A mountain lion was staring at him, its eyes glowing in the light of the headlamp. It slowly and deliberately circled the campsite, ready to pounce at any moment.

The hunter had a nice twist to the mountain lion story and told it well. His friend had seen a mountain lion attack an elk: "On a dead run the mountain lion jumped on the elk's back, dug its fangs into its neck and broke it in one motion." He looked at me to judge my reaction. "And you know how big elk are. He broke it just like that!" (Snapping his fingers) He glanced at me again. There was a look of frustration on his face. I wasn't giving him the reaction he was used to. (I'll say this for the guy. He wasn't a quitter.) "If a mountain lion can break an elk's neck that easy think what it could do to a hiker? Hell, a mountain lion's so quiet it would pounce on you and have you on the ground before you knew what hit you!"

I had a feeling he wouldn't stop until he got the appropriate reaction. "Wow! No kidding!"

"Yep. They're stone cold killers!"

I don't have a vivid enough imagination. I never gave much thought to mountain lions.

There were nearby forest fires caused by the thunderstorm. For the rest of the day the air was thick with smoke. I found a place to camp by a small lake just as it was getting dark. The only level spot was out in the open. I would have preferred to be under trees. It was bitterly cold. I had my gloves on and my fingers were freezing while I put up the tent. As I was closing my tent for the night I saw a fog rolling in. I was wearing everything and it was just enough to stay warm.

The next morning, condensation had frozen on the inside and outside of my tent. The condensation was so thick the tent crinkled as I rolled it up to put into its bag. It took a lot of fast hiking before I warmed up enough for my painfully cold hands to thaw out.

I spent much of the day hiking through beautiful forests and by small lakes. I was nearing Mt. Adams and the views should have been impressive. Once in a while I could see the outline of Mt. Adams through the thick smoke. There was a major fire on the other side of Mt. Adams and firefighters were closing some of the side trails. This had me worried. A shift in wind direction could close the Trail. A couple of weary, sooty, firefighters headed down the Trail carrying their axes.

Just before dark I found a great spot to camp at the base of Mt. Adams. It was twenty yards off of the Trail. A small pathway led to it. There was a flat, smooth area with a fire ring surrounded by logs. A little spring was twenty yards downhill. It was a cold night and by 7:30 I was in my sleeping bag calculating my mileage for the day - 22. This camping spot was hidden from the Trail and I was surprised when another hiker showed up. He was gregarious and we chatted as he set up his tent and cooked dinner. He was an Israeli who was on vacation. He was a section hiker who had never camped before. He made more food than he needed and offered me part of his Mountain House dinner. How could I refuse? We had been talking for over half an hour and I hadn't looked out of my tent. I had my headlamp on and saw the guy for the first time. He was huge. It's a good thing because he had a tent big enough for four people. I could only imagine how much his pack weighed. The Mountain House Lasagna was good and I went down to the spring and washed the dishes. It was the least I could do. Around two in the morning a bull elk was down by the spring and let out its piercing call. If you are not familiar with the call of an elk, it's like a high pitched scream and very loud. I could hear the Israeli start up from his sleeping bag. I'm sure he had never heard anything like that in his life. I chuckled to myself. We talked the next morning before heading our separate ways. He was a south bound hiker. He told me I would reach the Knife's Edge in a day and a half. He said it was scary and dangerous. I thanked him for the information but was thinking that it was dangerous in the eyes of an inexperienced section hiker and it was probably so easy it would be a joke.

I had never heard of the Knife's Edge because I never wanted to know what was ahead. I wanted to be surprised. The only reason I glanced at Halfmile's maps in the morning was to see where the water sources were. I rarely looked at terrain features. I didn't want to know elevation changes. The way I looked at it, to reach Canada I had to hike 2,660 miles. If the Trail meandered and circled and I hiked ten miles to cover five miles as the crow flies, it didn't matter. A lot of the time the meandering made the Trail more gentle as it wandered by areas with grand views. So many hikers were constantly cussing the Trail. To me that mile that others cussed was one mile closer to Canada.

The hiking during the day was hazy with smoke. On the other side of Mt. Adams, firefighters were fighting a fire that was out of control and would eventually close the Trail. The summer months had been dry in Washington and it was a record breaking fire year. Despite the smoke, I was hiking through beautiful country. I crossed canyons and valleys and meadows. Sometimes I would be in dense forest and an hour later be hiking above tree line looking down on canyons and valleys and meadows. Often I was hiking along the side of the mountain. I approached an area with steep drop-offs and loose footing. It was moderately challenging. This was probably the Knife's Edge the section hiker was talking about. PPPSSSHHH. The rookie!

I ended the day in one of the most gorgeous campsites of all. It was actually a horse camp which hikers weren't supposed to use. I hadn't seen any horses and I hadn't seen any other campsites so I took my chances. The sun was setting and the surrounding mountains were a watermelon red. The campsite was high on the mountain, above tree line, and in a meadow. If I had taken a picture with my tent in the foreground, sitting on tightly cropped green grass, with blue and red and yellow wildflowers dotting a rocky landscape that gently sloped down to a blue stream at the base of glacier covered, red tinged mountains; the picture would have been worthy of the cover of Backpacker Magazine. Did I take the picture? I'll bet you know the answer.

I sat outside in the darkness for a long time. It felt like I was on top of the world. I could hear the stream gently flowing and see the outline of the nearby mountain and a sky full of stars. I watched a falling star shoot across the sky.

The next day I entered the Goat Rocks area. This was mountain goat country. The mountains were covered with glaciers and the white, mountain goats blended right in. This was a popular area and rightfully so. Much of it was wide open country with unobstructed views. In the afternoon I was hiking along a rocky pathway above tree line and came to a glacier that was a couple of hundred feet long and steep enough to be challenging. Once I crossed the glacier and was back on the rocky pathway there were sweeping views of the mountain ranges. There was a trail to the peak of the nearest mountain but it didn't look like the Trail. The Trail took a turn to the left and what I saw stopped me in my tracks. My eyes followed a rocky ridge that was over a mile long. There were sheer drop-offs of hundreds of feet on both sides of the alarmingly narrow ridge. It was no more than ten feet wide and, in places, only three feet wide. The Knife's Edge!

I refused to believe this could be the Pacific Crest Trail. I backed away from the edge and hunkered down out of the wind behind some rocks. I took out my map. Sure enough, it was the Trail. Shit! I went over and looked at the drop off again. It frightened me. I headed back to my little protected area behind the rocks. I took out a Cliff Bar and tried to settle my nerves. I had another Cliff Bar. This was for real. There was no room for error.

I started heading down. The pathway wound and twisted within its three to ten foot width. Sometimes I would be heading straight toward the drop off as I descended over loose rocks. I hate descending over loose rocks! The rocks on the pathway varied. Sometimes it was flat, thin, shale about as long as a brick that was piled together. If one piece started to slide all the pieces would slide together. Sometimes it was shale and rocks the size of my fist. Other times it was rocks the size of gravel. All of it was loose. The key word was slide. As my feet were pushing off of the rocks some would slide over the side. It would start a rock slide that would tumble down the steep rocky surface of the mountain. I kept thinking: "That could be me." There were times the Trail was so steep and the rocks so loose, there was no way to keep from sliding down. It was a matter of controlling a three foot slide until I reached an area where I could stop the slide. I knew if I fell and lost control I would fall over the side. My hiking stick saved me more than once. When I would make it through a particularly precarious area I would stop and regroup.

I was high on the mountain looking down on almost everything. It felt like I was "King of the Mountain". There were nearby mountain ranges and far away ones. Most were full of glaciers. There were beautiful mountain lakes. Packwood Glacier was downhill to my left. It was huge. I scanned it for mountain goats but didn't see any.

Hiking along the Knife's Edge was nerve wracking and exhilarating. By the time I finished the most difficult part, endorphins were shooting through my body and I felt great. The pathway eventually widened but most of the time it still traveled along the ridge. Sometimes I could see the Trail, way in the distance, heading steeply around the side of a rock formation with sheer drop-offs. This was not an area for the faint of heart.

There was a picture on the cover of Yogi's PCT Handbook that caught my imagination. There were hikers in the foreground, descending the Trail on top of a sundrenched mountain. There was a shiny glacier on their right and a white capped volcano far in the distance. I didn't know where Yogi took the picture. For hundreds of miles, whenever I was high on a mountain, I tried to match the area I was hiking through with Yogi's picture. It never matched. All of a sudden I turned a corner and there was the picture. The Trail descended and I could visualize exactly where the hikers were on the pathway, with the glacier on the right and Mt. Rainier in the background. I stopped at the exact spot where Yogi took the picture. It was something I daydreamed about while planning my thru-hike. "I wonder if I'll see that view?" I did! Sadly, the area was too smoke filled to take a picture.

The beauty of the Knife's Edge and the surrounding area rivaled the beauty of the High Sierras. As I was walking along the ridge with magnificent views in every direction I kept saying over and over: "How lucky am I?"

The Trail swung to the right and gradually started to descend. The views stayed gorgeous. This was a rocky area with beautiful wildflowers. There were small glaciers next to the Trail and many little streams feeding into a rapidly flowing stream. The descent became steeper, rockier, and more slippery. When I was within five feet of an area where the Trail leveled out, I slipped and fell on my back. Fortunately the pack broke my fall and I bounced right back up. I laughed. I was grateful that hadn't happened while I was on the Knife's Edge.

Eventually I reached the tree line. There was an overlook to a vast valley below. The valley was completely filled with dense smoke. It looked like I would be descending into a fog. I was still one hundred feet above it and although I had an hour of daylight to work with, I started looking for a place to put my tent. Fortunately I didn't have to descend much further to find a lovely spot under an old pine tree. That night, smoke surrounded my tent and it was hard to take a full breath.

The smoke had cleared out the next morning and it wasn't too cold. It was a perfect morning for hiking. Within two hundred yards of where I camped I saw the most magnificent elk I have seen in my life. It had huge antlers. It was on the Trail about thirty feet away. When it saw me it instantly sprinted up the mountain, hardly making a sound. My goal for the day was to make it to White Pass and the Kracker Barrel convenience store that had my resupply box. When I was within eight miles of White Pass I talked with some section hikers who told me there was trail magic at the pass. That was enough to quicken my pace. This was a beautiful area for hiking and there were a lot of day hikers and section hikers enjoying it.

When I was within two miles of the trail magic I was stopped by a man and woman who asked if I was a thru-hiker. I could see the man wanted to talk. He had hiked this section of trail for many years and was dying to tell me about it. He was enthusiastic, sincere, and really trying to be helpful. I had a feeling if I cut him short I would hurt his feelings. I spent a good ten minutes as he named every side trail, picnic area, mountain, and stream in the area. I thought he was winding down and I could cut in and thank him for his valuable information, but before I could, he started talking about forest fires and wind directions. This wasn't going to end until I put a stop to it, so as he was drawing a breath, I stuck out my hand and thanked him profusely. His chest was puffed out as he and his wife headed up the Trail.

This happened many times. Section or day hikers who had a great love of the forest, were delighted to be hiking, had a vast knowledge of their local area, and were eager to share it. There was a look I could spot long before one of these enthusiasts said a word. I would groan inwardly when I would see the cheerful face and eye contact that was locked on like a laser guided missile. "Are you a thru-hiker?"

Yes...

"Just wait until you get to Trapper Ridge! You're going to love it! To get there you'll see Spark Plug Lake on your left, then Little Plug Lake, keep going and you'll pass Surprise Lake, there's some switchbacks to the top and you'll see Trap Lake to the west ...." They would give this detailed information assuming I knew what the hell they were talking about. I didn't! On a 2,660 mile journey I was lucky to know which National Park I was hiking in. I always tried to extricate myself as quickly and diplomatically as possible.

I finally made it to White Pass and Trail Magic. Lost and Found had a big screened tent surrounding all kinds of food, sodas, beer, and wine. She was a lady about my age who loved to hike and enjoyed the hiking community. She had hiked many trails over the years. I was greeted by Mother Goose. My first thought was: "How did she get ahead of me, again?" Unfortunately, her knee had gotten worse and forced her off the

Trail. I could see how disappointed she was. She had a train ticket back to Illinois in four days. In the mean time she was helping her friend, Lost and Found, with the trail magic.

We were the only people there. Lost and Found made me some hot broccoli, cheese, and rice soup. It was excellent. I told her that Spatula, Mismatch, and Pitstop should be right behind me and she started making some more. After half an hour they still hadn't shown up. I told Lost and Found they must have taken a shortcut to the Highway for a hitch into Packwood, Washington. Sure hate to see that excellent broccoli, cheese, and rice soup go to waste I hinted sincerely, trying not to show my eagerness. It worked! My little tummy was warm and happy.

We talked hiking for another hour before more hikers showed up. I headed to the Kracker Barrel to pick up my resupply box and headed back to the trail magic. Shack, Weeki, Tracks, Ninja, Green Machine, Chuckles, and Chatterbox were all there. I decided to stay the night. Most hikers started early the next morning but I stuck around and Lost and Found made me a hot breakfast.

She started giving trail magic two days earlier and a lot of people had signed her register. It was fun seeing all the names. The day before, U-Haul, Tangent, Holstein, Nate, Jenna, Jack Y Bean, Lil Dipper, and Gut Feeling signed the register. Nate and Jenna left the same day I arrived at White Pass. I missed them by five hours.

There were twelve names from the first day. I didn't know one name in that group. That meant I was catching up to them. After White Pass, there were few places for hikers to get off of the Trail. With their fitness, young bodies, and fewer distractions, they finally started making the miles they were capable of. I never caught up to one of the twelve hikers listed on the register from the first day.

U-Haul, Tangent, Holstein, Nate, Jenna, Jack Y Bean, Lil Dipper, Gut Feeling, Tracks, Ninja, Green Machine, Chuckles, Chatterbox, Spatula, Mismatch, and Pitstop eventually left me behind, too.

I thanked Lost and Found for the excellent trail magic, wished Mother Goose a speedy recovery, and headed on my way. By now it was 11:00 am. I was rested and energized and hiked twenty-four miles before calling it a day.

The next day the Trail clung tightly to the side of the mountain for miles. There were areas with steep drop offs. A couple of hikers were heading my way. As I looked at them it felt like I was in a time warp. I stopped to talk with them. They were brothers in their early sixties and were bubbling with happiness. They would talk at the same time and end each others sentences. They backpacked together for a week each year and had been doing this for many years. The first thing I said to them was. "You look like you stepped right out of the early seventies." They laughed and one of them said: "This is the same backpack I started with when I was eighteen years old in 1969. I have a picture in my living room, taken on that backpacking trip, wearing this backpack." Both brothers were wearing blue jeans, long sleeved plaid shirts, waffle stomper boots, boonie hats, and external frame backpacks with the aluminum tubing. This hike was a trip down memory lane for them. Except for their paunches and grey beards they looked exactly like they would have in the late sixties and early seventies.

Back then lightweight backpacking didn't exist. It was a status symbol to carry fifty pounds or more in your backpack. To start a conversation one of the first questions was: "How much are you carrying in that pack?" Casually: "Oh - 70 pounds." Instant respect. If you were carrying less than fifty pounds you were a wuss.

An hour later I was back in a forest so thick with trees it felt like I was hiking in a green tunnel. I came to a river with a good flow and tried to find the best way to get across without getting wet. I tried walking about halfway across on a big log and realized that wasn't going to work. I looked upstream and downstream searching for rocks to hop over. That didn't look promising. To Hell with it. I picked the shallowest area and sloshed through. It was a little over my knees. When I reached the other side I noticed Shack and Weeki for the first time. They had been quietly watching my decision making with amusement. I noticed that their shoes were wet, too. They were taking a break and heating some food. Shack was slumped against a downed tree looking totally exhausted. The man just kept plugging away. I would have to put him up there with U-Haul for sheer determination.

The forest was so shady and thick with vegetation that within a two hour period I saw a deer, two elk, and a small bear. I just saw the rear end of the bear as it went crashing through the forest. The deer was swift and quiet as it bounded away. It hardly seemed to touch the downed branches. The elk banged into large fallen branches making their exit. It was loud and sounded painful.

In the afternoon I was stopped by a southbound hiker with another external frame backpack. His name was Mark Trail. He was a thru-hiker doing a flip-flop. He hiked the PCT northbound for part of his hike and then traveled to the Canadian border and headed southbound to the place he ended northbound.

Hikers flip-flopped if they didn't think they would make it to Canada before the snow. He had been hiking southbound for the last two weeks and had taken a video of every northbound thru-hiker he crossed paths with. He took a video of me and I answered a couple of questions for the audio portion. He had already interviewed twenty-two hikers. He said it was the most thru-hikers he had seen in one day since he started hiking from the Canadian border. I realized I had finally caught up to the "Herd" that started after the PCT Kickoff on April 29th. I was now part of "The Herd". Mark was proud of his Jansport Frame Backpack that he called Old Blue. I wondered at the probability of seeing three external framed backpacks in one day. I hadn't seen more than five the whole hike. The only answer I could come up with: "It must be like, Karma, man."

It was dark by the time I found a campsite three hundred yards from a small lake where campers were set up illegally. They had an elk horn and were trying to make elk calls. Their calls were pathetic, which they found hilarious. I had a feeling they were either very drunk or very stoned.

It was cold when I started the next morning but it turned into a warm delightful day. I was camped only a few miles from a highway with a big parking lot. It was Sunday morning and heading to the highway I passed a lake that was loaded with campers. When I reached the parking lot almost all the parking spaces were filled. This was a popular area for a good reason. The hiking was challenging and gorgeous. It was the 16th of September and autumn colors were starting to show.

I passed a lot of hikers enjoying the beauty of our national parks. I spent a good part of the day hiking up to passes and then following the rocky, treeless, pathway along the sides of mountains for miles. It was a smoky day but I could see Mt. Rainier looming through the haze. I remember first seeing it way back near Timberline Lodge. It was impressive even then but far in the distance. Now I was as close as I would get to it. It was Huge! From Oregon all the way to Canada it was a reference point on the horizon. It gave me a sense of the scope of my hike. First, it was far ahead and small on the horizon. As I continued hiking it got bigger and bigger until it filled the horizon. Then it was behind me and gradually decreased in size as I continued hiking for the next three hundred miles. Even as I neared Canada, it was still the dominant mountain.

I finished the day with twenty-three miles and worked hard to get them. On my calendar that night I wrote my total miles - 2,360. I also put down the number 300 and circled it - three hundred miles to go. I was starting the countdown. I put down the number 11. That was the number of days I thought I had to the end of the hike. It was a bit too optimistic but I didn't know it at the time. I would revise the "days to go" number, three more times before the hike ended.

The next day was long and grinding. The surrounding mountains had dirt roads leading to mining pits. There were logging roads and areas that had been harvested for lumber. It was more of a day to get through and make miles and I ended with twenty-six smoke filled miles. The only highlight was a terrific camping spot on top of the highest mountain. There were views as far as I could see. The sun was setting through the dense smoke creating a blood red sunset. It was a perfectly still night. There were no streams nearby and it was eerily quiet - absolutely no sound. I sat perfectly still and enjoyed it.

The next morning there was an equally impressive sunrise. It was a tough day of hiking. The sign at one of the intersections was so confusing I had to get out my GPS and Halfmile's map. In California and Oregon, at a trail junction, often a sign would have PCT and a directional arrow. I would see the arrow and not even break stride. A lot of the trail signs in Washington were not geared to PCT hikers and many times were confusing. Sometimes hikers would make a bad choice and head miles out of their way. Whenever I would come to a confusing intersection I would take out my GPS and set it to the next waypoint. If the arrow pointed to the right I would take the pathway to the right. When I first started using my GPS in California I kept it on all day and would be constantly monitoring the miles hiked and my average speed with and without breaks. By the time I reached Washington I used it only a couple of times a day for navigation and less than a minute each time. Those minutes were invaluable. It felt great knowing my exact location and which way I needed to go.

I ended the day by a small lake a couple of miles before Snoqualmie Pass Ski Resort. On my calendar that night I wrote: "Tough day of hiking. I'm tired. Ready to go to bed." I had been pushing the pace as I planned. My mileage since leaving Cascade Locks, Oregon was: 23, 24, 22, 25.5, 22.5,14 at White Pass, 24, 23, 26, and 24.This was difficult hiking. My body was handling the workload better than I hoped but by the time I hit a trail town I was ready for a break. Snoqualmie Pass Ski Resort was the next trail stop and I was looking forward to a resupply and big breakfast. I made it to breakfast by 8:00 the next morning. After resupplying and a huge breakfast, I was back on the Trail by 10:00 am.

It was Wednesday, September 19th. I needed to make it to Skykomish, Washington in order to pick up my resupply box at the Post Office by Saturday at its 10:00 am closing time. If I didn't make it by 10:00 am, I would have to wait until Monday. Once I made it to Stevens Pass then I had a twenty mile hitch to Skykomish. The distance from Snoqualmie Pass to Stevens Pass was seventy-five miles. Since I was getting a late start I was going to try to get as many miles as possible on Wednesday and hike a minimum of twenty-five miles a day for the next two days. If there was any difference to make up I would get up extra early on Saturday morning to reach Steven's Pass by 8:00 am. The Trail between Snoqualmie Pass and Stevens Pass was supposed to be spectacular but very challenging.

It started with a long, steady, climb along the side of the mountain. As I hiked I was looking across a deep canyon at a tall mountain with many glaciers. There were streams created by the glaciers and water was raging down the streams. I could see white foam as the water crashed over rocks.

Sometimes a stream would have three or four waterfalls as the water steeply descended to the canyon floor. The waterfalls were far in the distance but I could hear them flowing. Near the top of the mountain, for about two hundred feet, the Trail had been blasted right into the rock. There were sheer drop-offs and beautiful views. This was a popular area that section hikers told me about on two separate occasions. Hikers were out in force. The hiking along the edge of the mountain continued for a long time. There was a lot of loose rock on the Trail and I had to take my time to keep from falling. The Trail continued to climb and headed into a full, healthy forest.

Near the top as I was taking a break by a small pond, two hikers caught up to me and stopped to talk. They were a couple in their mid-forties and hiking the section between Snoqualmie Pass and Stevens Pass. They were so enthusiastic. After 2,430 miles and hiking almost every day for four and a half months I was still having a great time but was kind of jaded. It would take Crater Lake, Tunnel Falls, or the Knife's Edge to reach their level of enthusiasm. I picked up on their energy. They gave me a pâté on crackers and an apple. This was a roller coaster day of steep ups and downs often passing clear, blue, lakes. I only made seventeen miles.

I started extra early the next morning knowing I had to make big miles. The Trail was so rocky and dangerous, with steep drop-offs, that I had to hike cautiously for most of the day. It was a very tiring day and I only made twenty-one miles. It was frustrating.

I started hiking the next day at sunrise. I was trying for a thirty mile day. It was super frustrating! The Trail in some places was so steep, rocky, and dangerous, that I couldn't make the miles. I knew I had to stay within my ability and on loose rock, sometimes one mile an hour was as fast as I could go. By 6:00 pm I had only hiked fifteen exhausting miles. I was weary and still had twenty-three miles to get to Stevens Pass by the next morning.

I was very conflicted. I will try to give you an idea of how my mind was working. One part was saying: "I need to get this thru-hike completed. The weather isn't going to hold out forever. What if I came all this way only to be snowed in before reaching Canada? I can't afford a delay. If I don't make it to the Post Office by Saturday at 10:00 am I'm going to have to sit around twiddling my thumbs for the rest of Saturday, ALL day Sunday, then wait for the Post Office to open on Monday, sort out my resupply package, hitchhike twenty miles back to the Trail and probably not get started until noon on Monday, and that's if I'm lucky enough to get a ride. If I can make it to the Post Office by 10:00 am Saturday I can resupply, have a good lunch, and be back hiking the same afternoon. Not to mention saving money on a motel room and extra meals. I've got to make Steven's Pass tomorrow morning by 8:00 at the latest. Starting now, I have fifteen hours of hiking to make twenty-three miles. That's less than two miles an hour. I can do that."

The other part was saying: "I'm tired. I've been hiking since 6:00 this morning - that's twelve hours. Now I want to hike fifteen more hours? In the dark? Over Trail that will probably continue to be rocky and treacherous? Is this safe? I haven't spent much time night hiking and when I have my hiking stick has saved me from a lot of falls. As I hike into the night and get even more tired what if I fall and get seriously injured? I'm only two hundred miles from the finish. Is this worth the risk?"

My mind was in "go" mode and I hiked into the night with my headlamp showing the pathway in front of me. After an hour the weariness started to set in. I stumbled on a rock, sharply jammed my hiking stick into the ground to break my fall, and started looking for a place to camp. Fortunately a good spot showed up in less than fifteen minutes.

The next day there were some treacherous areas. I was glad not to have hiked them in the dark. In the morning I traveled along the top of a mountain where clouds below me came almost to my feet. The cloud layer extended as far as I could see. It almost felt like I could do a swan dive into the fluffy clouds and they would envelope me in their softness.

There was a stream crossing that was the hardest of my hike. Mismatch was already at the stream waiting for Spatula and Pitstop. I reached the stream and looked back to see Spatula heading down the steep pathway. He was talking to Mismatch as he navigated the big, loose, gnarly, rocks. He wasn't even looking down. Amazing!

The stream was being fed by a nearby glacier. The water careened steeply downhill and was loud. The stream was only thirty feet wide but the water was moving far too fast to wade across. Thirty feet downstream were huge boulders. The water funneled and crashed into them. Ten feet downstream there were rocks sticking out of the water big enough to stand on. They were spaced so I could rock hop ten feet towards the far side. Some were wet and looked slippery but they were wide enough to take a chance. If I jumped to a rock and slipped off, my feet wouldn't touch the streambed. The current was so fast I would be swept downstream into the boulders. It was tricky staying balanced as I hopped from one rock to the next. I made it to a thick branch that headed upstream and angled ten feet closer to the far bank. The branch was wedged between rocks and looked like it had been there for quite a while, but it was wobbly. I grabbed onto the branch and climbed onto it. I was climbing upstream on all fours trying to keep my balance on the slippery branch. Water was shooting by on both sides. My body was close to the water and I was getting sprayed when the water hit nearby rocks. Once I made it to the end of the branch the water smoothed out and I was able to wade, knee deep, to the other side. While I crossed, Mismatch was shouting encouragement and pointing out areas he thought had the best possibilities. Whew! I wanted this hike to be an adventure but that was a bit much! I couldn't imagine doing that at night. I watched Pitstop, Mismatch, and Spatula, cross the stream. We each chose a different route.

I reached Steven's Pass at 8:00 pm. I attempted to hitchhike but cars were zooming up and over the pass and didn't see me until it was too late to stop. It was dark and chilly. I could see my breath. I felt very much alone. As I had my thumb out, I was thinking: "It's Saturday night. It's too dark to see who is inside the car. What are you doing out here?" I headed back to the Trail and backtracked half a mile to a camping spot that I remembered. It was in a rocky area and picas woke me the next morning with their whistles.

I reached Steven's Pass at 8:00 am and was lucky enough to be picked up by the fourth car. He actually burned rubber coming to a halt. I reached the little railroad town of Skykomish, Washington at 8:30 am just in time for the all you can eat breakfast at the Cascadia Inn Café. There were six other hikers at the cafe and I joined them at a large table. The waitress filled my coffee cup and I headed to the buffet. There was a popular hiker hostel a few miles from Skykomish run by Jerry and Andrea Dinsmore. Just then, seventeen hikers who had stayed at the Dinsmore's descended on the cafe. Here were twenty-three skinny, ravenous, thru-hikers descending on this little cafe like a swarm of locusts. The poor cook. She was doing an outstanding job trying to keep the trays full of food, but there were times when hikers were milling around waiting for the next batch to arrive. When it did they would swarm all over it. The food was excellent. I had ten small cinnamon rolls that were out of this world. I held my own with the young hikers and filled my plate six times before I was full. There were benches and chairs in front of the Cascadia Inn and I talked with some locals as I relaxed and digested the wonderful food. Rooms became available an hour later and I took my first zero since visiting the Pryor's over three months earlier. The Cascadia Inn was built in 1922 and had a lot of character. My room was spacious and clean and all the fixtures were new. The first thing I did was take a deep, hot, bath. Aaahhhh! When I finished the bathwater was so dirty I cleaned the tub. The owner was friendly and helpful and let me use his cell phone to make some phone calls. I even reached Johanna. That was a pleasure. I spent the rest of the day eating and relaxing. Railroad tracks were within twenty yards of the Cascadia Inn. A couple of times in the night the blare of a train horn was so loud I sat up in bed like the Israeli hiker but I was easily back asleep in no time. By the time I left Skykomish the next morning I was clean, rested, full of food, and glad to have taken a zero day.

While I was in Skykomish, I met Blackbeard and Destroyer. They were a couple in their late twenties from England. I asked them what the weather looked like for the next few days. They told me there was not supposed to be any rain for the next ten days. That was great news. My luck was still holding. In my hotel room I had taken out my maps and planned for the rest of the journey. I planned to push hard and finish in eight days.

It was 104 miles from Skykomish to my next stop, Stehekin, Washington. Unlike heading into the High Sierras and having heard so much about them beforehand, I knew nothing about the North Cascade Mountains and the Glacier Peak Wilderness. Was I in for a treat! It was the closest I have ever come to true wilderness.

I hiked eleven miles the first day before putting up my tent in the dark. It was a cold night and the wind was howling through the trees. I heard Lava Goat and Mark pass my tent in the night which made me happy to be in my warm sleeping bag.

I followed their shoe prints all the next day - Mark's size 14 Cascadia sevens and Lava Goat's size 9 Cascadia six's. I didn't see one hiker the whole day. I had the wilderness to myself. The colors were stunning. The green grass on the mountainsides had turned a soft shade of yellow. Huckleberry bushes were in various stages of purple, red, and brown. Patches of lupine were still blue and fragrant. The red and sometimes orange indian paint was holding its color. Firs and pines filled the countryside with green. Western Larch provided a brilliant yellow. The hiking was difficult but fun. There were still patches of blueberries that were juicy and delicious. Nearing the top of a mountain I startled an owl eating a dead rabbit. It took off but the little rabbit was on its side staring at me with its blank eye. I camped high on a ridge. I stopped an hour early to enjoy the beauty of my surroundings. I set up the tent at a leisurely pace and watched the sun sink slowly below the mountain. It was quiet and peaceful. I realized I didn't have many of these nights left and was going to miss them.

The next morning I passed colonies of marmots with their little dens covering the hillside. They were used to hikers and went about their business. Blackbeard and Destroyer caught up to me and we spent a couple of hours hiking together. Over the next few days we would leapfrog and spend time talking as we hiked. They were both genuinely nice people. They had the gift of gab and a spontaneous sense of humor. This was a trip of a lifetime for them. Destroyer quit her job to hike the PCT knowing it wouldn't be there for her when she returned. With her happy, optimistic outlook on life, I felt she would have no problem finding a job when she returned home. I chuckled every time I heard her trail name - Destroyer. She was anything but. She had a high voice and a British accent and was disgustingly mild mannered. I never heard Destroyer or Blackbeard ever put other hikers down. After I had been around Destroyer for a while the cynic in me came out: "She can't be this nice. C'mon. Put somebody down. I want to hear a little gossip. Gripe about something. C'mon. Give me some dirt!" It never happened.

Sometimes when you are hiking alone you have too much time to think. I imagined this scenario:

Destroyer is attending her first meeting of the villain society. Roll call is being taken: (If you are reading this out loud, put on your gravelly voice and try to sound as much like Hulk Hogan as possible.)

AVENGER! .... YEA!

TERMINATOR! .... YO!

BRUISER! .... YEA!

KILLER! .... HERE!

DESTROYER!

DESTROYER!! Oh….Hellew (Give it your best Julie Andrews voice.)

The hiking was difficult but it kept getting better by the day. Just like in the High Sierras and the Hundred Mile Wilderness, I was awed by the beauty. I knew I had at least a ten day window of good weather so I decided to slow down and enjoy it.

The next day was a day of vistas. I spent a good part of it hiking steeply up and down mountains. On one long climb I spent more than an hour taking switchbacks to the top. I stopped on a small saddle and looked down on a vast rocky canyon whose sides were towering glacier covered mountains. There were streams and waterfalls and a river on the canyon floor. Before heading down I took a break on the little saddle. I was admiring the view when I heard the sound of something heading my way at great speed. I looked up over my shoulder and a falcon shot by on a steep descent completely focused on its prey in the valley. Its wings were tucked in   and   it   was   perfectly   aerodynamic: WWWHHHEEEEEEEEHHHHHWW.

It missed me by about ten feet but would have knocked me senseless if it had hit me. Falcons can reach speeds up to 200 miles an hour on a descent and this one was in that range. The sound was loud and startling.

As the Trail switch backed down the mountain and headed to the river it passed little ponds surrounded by tight, velvet like, grass. At the river the Trail veered to the left and entered another wide, pine filled, valley. I caught up to a man hiking with his dog. He was on a weeklong backpacking trip. He had a Yellow Lab who was welcoming, friendly, and wanted badly to be petted. I obliged.

The next two days were spent hiking through old growth forest. For the past few years, because the bridge over the Suiattle River had been destroyed in a flood, hikers crossed the river on a log that had fallen across the river. It was five feet above the rapidly flowing river and was a dangerous crossing. A new bridge was completed in 2011. Seven miles of new Trail were also added. The builders spared no expense. It was a wide, well- built Trail. It almost felt like a boulevard. The bridge was high above the water so it couldn't be knocked out by floods. Some hikers still used the old log crossing. It saved a few miles but was probably more for the adrenaline.

On the new Trail I passed a forest of giant cedars. The forest was full of vegetation and seemed almost marshy at times. One of the cedars had fallen across the Trail. Trail maintainers cut a block out of the tree as wide as the pathway. Someone counted the tree rings. The tree was 658 years old. It was a seedling in 1355.

There were many trees much wider than this one that had to have been over a thousand years old. This area was in a storm track and normally the wettest part of the PCT. It was full of glaciers and perennial snow fields which added to its beauty. After crossing the bridge there was a long, steep, uphill grade with a lot of long switchbacks to get to the top. By the end of the day I was exhausted.

The next morning my weary body was moving slowly. I was hiking through old growth forest. There were many giant cedars and I was constantly searching for the widest and oldest. Eventually, I reached a river. I had to head upstream for a couple of hundred yards before I found a long old log that crossed the river.

As I got further into this thru-hike my agility and confidence improved. I scampered over the log. The pathway mellowed and followed the river. The water was crystal clear - pristine. There were colorful leaves in some of the shallow areas which sparkled in the morning sun. The water was flowing at a leisurely pace and where it pooled I could see small fish. I walked at a leisurely pace enjoying the autumn colors. I eventually picked up the pace to make it to a camping spot just before High Bridge and a bus ride into Stehekin the next morning.

About five miles before High Bridge, and right next to the Trail, I startled an animal at the base of a large tree that had its nose in a squirrel's den. I was only five feet from it. It shot five feet up the tree and stopped at eye level. We stared at each other. It looked like a monkey, with its slender body and long curved tail. It had a face more like a cat. I had never seen anything like it. It looked me right in the eye and didn't seem afraid. I almost felt like I was being challenged: "Your move." I was fascinated but realized I was too close and moved away. There was a Forest Service office in Stehekin and I couldn't wait to ask a Forest Ranger what kind of animal I had seen.

I was looking forward to Stehekin, Washington. I had read so many good things about it from the journals of previous hikers. I knew I had to take a zero in Stehekin because I would arrive Sunday morning and the Post Office with my resupply box wouldn't be open until Monday. Stehekin was the last trail town before reaching Canada and it was perfect. It was next to beautiful Lake Chelan. Tall mountains surrounded the lake. There were no roads to Stehekin. The only way to get there was by boat. It was a popular tourist attraction but by September 30th the tourist season was winding down. Ferries brought a few buses and cars to Stehekin for the locals and I was picked up at High Bridge and driven five miles to Stehekin.

Before reaching Stehekin, we stopped at a small organic farm not more than two acres in size. It had a garden with high fences to keep out the animals. There were giant sunflowers, cornstalks, tomato plants, squash, lettuce, chard, pole beans, and kale. There was a goat pen behind the little farmhouse. Goat cheese and goat yogurt were for sale. The owner was a fit, tanned, man, in his early sixties. He had a long ponytail, worn, callused, hands, and was barefoot. He had been living on this little plot of land since the late sixties. He traveled by bike or foot. He was living exactly the life he wanted, a simple life off of the land. I purchased some goat cheese which was excellent, plums that couldn't have been juicier, and herb flavored tortilla chips which I crushed and added to my trail mix giving it an extra zing.

When we reached Stehekin the bus stopped in front of a small grocery store and a restaurant. I had to climb some wooden stairs to get to the terrace. Standing in front of the restaurant on the deck overlooking Lake Chelan I was standing where hundreds of other thru-hikers had been. There is a picture in Yogi's Guidebook where she and seven other hikers were leaning against a rail and smiling for the camera. They looked relaxed and happy. I placed myself in that group picture, standing right where they had stood. It was a great feeling.

I heard from one of the hikers there was free camping in a campground only a quarter of a mile away and I could register at the Forest Service office. I headed over. I was dying to ask about the little animal I had seen. The Forest Ranger was friendly and helpful. After I gave her a description, she said: "That sounds like a pine martin - let me check." She brought out a book and rifled through the pages. "Is this it?" It sure is. She reserved a spot for me in the campground and I headed over. It was a shady little campground right on the hillside under old oak trees. I set up my tent, left my gear inside, and headed to the restaurant to meet Symbiosis for lunch.

I first met Symbiosis in Skykomish. He was a section hiker who started at Santium Pass just outside of Sisters, Oregon. Once he made it to the Canadian border he would have hiked all of the Pacific Crest Trail. We leapfrogged almost all the way to the Canadian border. He hiked hellacious hours, often hiking far into the night, cowboy camping even on the coldest nights, and hiking before dawn the next morning. I enjoyed talking with a person nearer my age. He finished the same day I did and his delight at having finished the journey was just as genuine as mine. This man lived for hiking. He was super enthusiastic. Over the years he had met some of the hiking legends and knew their hiking styles, what they ate, and what made them successful. I learned a lot from him. He looked to be in his early forties. When he told me he was sixty I was amazed. He was waiting for my amazed reaction and received it with satisfaction. After spending time with him I noticed he mentioned his age quite often and enjoyed the inevitable reaction. Unlike stuff-your-face thru-hikers, he had a strict, healthy diet. When he would see me putting away junk food I wouldn't consider eating at home, I could see him cringe. He attempted a couple of times to advocate for healthy eating but I was convinced everything I put into my mouth was going toward energy and didn't have a chance to stick around in my body and do damage. Was I wrong! When I returned home and had a cholesterol test a week later my cholesterol had jumped thirty-three points!

Many hikers talked about living a simple lifestyle without all the "material" things to complicate and clutter their lives. Symbiosis talked the talk and walked the walk. He didn't own a car. His transportation was his bicycle which kept him fit. He was an engineer who was self-employed. While he was hiking he was working full time. He would have his computer sent to a town up the Trail. When he reached the town he would stay at a motel for two or three days and work on projects related to his business. When he was finished he would send his computer to a town further up the Trail and continue his hike. He made good money but lived simply. He was a Pacific Crest Trail Guardian, having contributed a sum between $1,000 and $2,649. This was his lifestyle. After finishing his hike of the Pacific Crest Trail he was planning to hike the Appalachian Trail the same way.

During my thru-hike I had many hours alone with my thoughts. I was rarely bored while hiking. There were days when the hiking was difficult and I had to stay completely focused. There were days when the scenery was so beautiful I spent the whole day enjoying it. Most days there were times when I could let my mind wander. I didn't try to control my thoughts. I just let them float into my mind. I could follow a thought, free of distractions, for as long as I wanted. This gave me a chance to clarify how I want to live my life.

I think my lifestyle is closer to that of Symbiosis. I want to keep my life simple. Over the years I have been getting rid of possessions. I want to keep the things I need and those that have good memories.

Good friends, interesting conversations, invigorating walks, volunteering – these are the things that give me pleasure.

I have all the things I need or want but many people don't. During the Christmas holidays, Public Service Company of New Mexico will match my donation to help heat the homes of the very poor in New Mexico. They give priority to the elderly. Heifer International has a goal of ending hunger and poverty in a sustainable way. They will both get a donation during the holiday.

I have enjoyed hiking and backpacking all my life. Now that I have hiked the Appalachian Trail and Pacific Crest Trail, I enjoy it even more.

When I am hiking I am away from the comforts of home where I can turn on the air conditioner when I'm too warm or turn up the heater if I'm too cold. I am a part of nature where I experience, intensely, the desert heat, my throat parched from lack of water, pelting sandy winds, a brilliant star filled night listening to the mournful howl of a coyote and not another person within miles, sweat soaked climbs that go on forever, biting black flies, towering canyon walls, high mountain passes with gorgeous views, sparkling mountain lakes, rocky pathways with sheer drop-offs, majestic glacier covered volcanoes, thundering waterfalls, a pine martin staring me down, the piercing call of an elk, clear mountain streams, bone chilling cold, and a marmot peeping into my tent to see if everything is ok.

Is this fun? Hell Yes! When I'm hiking I feel truly alive. It really is an addictive lifestyle. There will be many hikes in my future. The next one will be the 3,000 plus mile Continental Divide Trail. It is supposed to be wild and rugged. I can't wait!

If I am fortunate enough to complete the Continental Divide Trail, I will be one of fewer than 150 thru-hikers to have completed the Triple Crown, and probably one of only a handful to have done all of the hikes in his sixties. The Triple Crown is thru-hiking the Appalachian Trail, Pacific Crest Trail, and Continental Divide Trail.

I am thankful to live in a country that gives me the freedom to live the life I want to live. I have the time. I'm healthy. Look out, Mother Goose, with your 36,000 plus hiking miles. Here comes Jim, with 4,838 miles and counting!

After lunch I contacted Doug to let him know I had eighty miles to go and would probably be finishing by October 4th. Doug was my logistics man. He started researching bus and train fares from Manning Park, Canada to Vancouver, Canada and then Vancouver to Seattle, Washington. He also started researching plane fares from Seattle to Albuquerque. By the time I reached Manning Park, Doug had all the options for me. On short notice he found a great deal on a flight from Seattle to Albuquerque and purchased a ticket. Symbiosis had a much shorter flight and paid almost twice as much. Many thanks, Doug.

I headed back to my tent for some rest. Blackbeard and Destroyer were also at the campground and I asked them about the weather. They told me there was no rain in the forecast until the 13th of October. Great! But that a cold front was coming through and it would be turning cold. Not so great.

The next morning I had breakfast with Symbiosis and headed to the Post Office. Along with my resupply box, there was a box from Johanna containing a shirt and underwear to help ease my transition back into society, and another great letter. Those letters were always morale lifters. By 11:00 am I was back on the bus to High Bridge.

The last eighty miles from Stehekin to the border was the Pacific Crest

Trail at its best. Such a variety of terrain. The fall colors were in their full glory. Often I was high in the mountains with superb views. The hiking was challenging with a lot of climbs and descents. I leapfrogged with Blackbeard and Destroyer for much of the day. We hiked together for a while and they told me the Gourmet story. The first time I heard this story was at the trail magic at White Pass. I heard it many more times. It created anxiety but also provided focus. It became very real to us the closer we came to the finish. Gourmet was six miles from the Canadian border and the completion of his 2,660 mile thru-hike when he fell and broke his ankle. He was hiking alone and managed to drag himself to a clearing where he activated his Spot emergency locator beacon. A helicopter picked him up and flew him to a hospital in Seattle. We all groaned for the poor guy. In my book he earned thru-hiker status but there will always be the little * (Broken ankle six miles from the finish.)

That night I camped deep in a thick forest. The cold front moved in and it was very cold. Joyce sent me some thick mittens which I picked up at White Pass and this was the first time I needed them. I was wearing my balaclava and had the hood of my sleeping bag cinched so tightly I had only a couple of inches to breathe through. Blackbeard said it was supposed to get down to 17 degrees during the night and it felt like it did. The cold found spots on my body that were the least protected and exploited them. I had two socks on each foot and it wasn't enough. I spent a lot of the night trying to keep my toes warm without much success.

The next morning was painfully cold. I didn't even change out of my sleeping clothes because they were warmer than my hiking clothes. My regular gloves were covered by thick mittens and my hands were still freezing. The early morning hiking was along the side of a mountain that shielded the sun. I hiked for two painful hours before finally walking into sunlight. The rays of the sun hitting my body felt wonderful. I stopped and turned toward the sun and didn't move for ten minutes as I felt my frozen body begin to thaw. It was still cold by the time I made it to Rainy Pass. Robo Knee and Sea Hag had been giving trail magic for the last two days and were getting ready to leave. Chimney Sweep and Lorax, a couple of brothers I had been leapfrogging with for the last one hundred miles, were ahead of me and fortunately arrived at Rainy Pass just before Robo Knee and Sea Hag took off. By the time I arrived they were eating hot dogs, chips, cookies, and sipping hot chocolate. They were definitely happy hikers. Robo Knee and Sea Hag still had a lot of food left and each of us had at least three hot dogs with chili, two cups of hot chocolate, and I had three cups of strong coffee. All the food, hot coffee, and hot chocolate, warmed my body and I started to gain some badly needed energy. I met Robo Knee and Sea Hag back in the desert when they were hiking the California section of the PCT, and again in the High Sierras. They were in their early sixties and were fit and steady hikers. It was a pleasant surprise seeing them at Rainy Pass and their trail magic was much appreciated.

Blackbeard and Destroyer soon joined us. It was fun to see the delight on their faces when they saw us seated on camp chairs, eating hot dogs, and drinking hot chocolate, knowing they were next to be served. As we were talking I learned that Chimney Sweep had lived in Albuquerque, New Mexico. There was a long climb out of Rainy Pass and I hiked with the brothers for the next three hours. We had an interesting conversation. While we were climbing I had to work hard at it but I could stay at their pace. When we finally reached the top and started to descend the brothers shot ahead of me. They looked back and slowed down to let me catch up. I told them that on down hills I would be going very slowly and to hike at their own pace.

It began to snow in the afternoon. I watched snowflakes gently floating down the side of the mountain in the still air. I saw blue sky in the distance and an hour later was back in the sunshine. I found a camping spot next to a stream. By the time I had my tent set up it was already dark. I looked at my watch and it wasn't even 7:00 pm. I hiked twenty-two miles and worked hard to get it. Because of the cold, I hadn't had much sleep the night before. I was drowsy and after eating and taking care of camp chores I fell into a deep sleep.

HOOO! HOOO! HOOO!

I woke with a start! My adrenaline was pumping! What the hell was that?

Two bozo's were night hiking and this was their way of communicating. One guy was twenty feet from my tent and hooting at the top of his lungs. There were owl hoots in the distance. The hooting continued for the next fifteen minutes until they were out of range.

The temperature was down in the teens again in the night. I couldn't get warm enough. Now I had three socks on each foot and my feet were still cold. I realized I needed to get this hike over with.

My water bottles were frozen the next morning and the little stream was frozen. I needed to be hiking fast from the start to get circulation into my frozen toes and fingers. I pushed my weary sleep deprived body. I should have been miserable but the beauty of my surroundings wouldn't allow it.

While I was hiking along the side of the mountain I could see a marmot's den a hundred feet in the distance. As I got closer I could hear the marmot giving me a warning. The marmot was beside his den. The den was only three feet from the Trail on the uphill side. By the time I reached the den he would be looking down on me. As I got closer his warnings became louder and more frequent. It might be my imagination but I'm almost sure the pitch became higher. The little guy was standing his ground. I wasn't too worried. I had seen this too many times before. I thought of it as the Deputy Barney Fife Syndrome. There were three stages:

Stage #1: False bravado.

Stage #2: "Oh. Oh. What do I do now?" (This was accompanied with a visibly shaking body.)

Stage #3: Exit.

"Don't come any closer! I'm warning you!"

"Not One Step Closer! I Mean It! See These Ferocious Teeth? They're Not Just For Cracking Nuts! Any Closer And I Will Pounce On You!"

Shoo, little marmot. Back into your den.

"WHO ARE YOU TALKIN' TO? ARE YOU TALKIN' TO ME? HUH? ARE YOU TALKIN' TO ME??" "I AIN'T MOVIN' AN INCH! I'LL FIGHT YOU TO THE.......uh.....to the......I'm going back into my den, now....." ZOOM!

In the afternoon I reached Harts Pass. It was thirty miles from the border. Hikers who didn't have a passport and couldn't enter Canada planned to hike to the border, turn around, and head back the thirty miles to Hart's Pass. They planned to hitchhike on the seldom used mountain road to a town big enough to catch a bus to Seattle. I had planned to hike back to Hart's Pass, too. It seemed the least expensive travel option to get to Seattle and a plane back to Albuquerque. I gave up that idea when I contacted Doug in Stehekin about my travel options. When I reached Hart's Pass, I realized there was no way in hell I was going to hike thirty miles to the border then thirty miles back over the same route. A lot of hikers did, though.

This was a day of strenuous hiking. I climbed high to the tops of mountains, took switchbacks deep into canyons, passed mountain lakes, some with ice still in them, and followed rocky, switchbacks to mountaintops with more gorgeous views. I hiked twenty-five miles. I set up my tent in the dark next to a gently flowing stream. It was cold out and I had a feeling it was going to be a very cold night. I tried to stay warm but couldn't. Three toes on my left foot never warmed up in the night and were frozen and painful to walk on the next morning. It was so cold the only way I can describe it is "cussing cold." My whole body was covered with clothes. My gloves were covered by thick mittens. My balaclava covered my face so just my eyes were showing, and it was painfully cold. Every step was jarring and hurt. I cussed with each step. It felt better to cuss loudly! It took a good two hours to get some feeling into the three toes and finally start to warm up. Once I began to warm up I started to enjoy the day. It was a bright, sunny, day. The air was smoke free and the sky a deep blue. By the afternoon I was wearing a short sleeved shirt. I had to hike twenty-two miles to get to the border before dark, so I couldn't dawdle. The terrain was gentle and the hiking was easy. A feeling of fall was in the air. It was a perfect last day.

My body was tired. My feet now ached with every step. I knew I couldn't take much more of the cold night time temperatures. I hadn't had a rejuvenating sleep in days, but I was still enjoying seeing glaciers, fall colors, waterfalls, long narrow canyons, and so much more and I didn't want it to end.

I felt pride and satisfaction at having made it this far and the eager anticipation of reaching my goal. My main feeling this day was happiness.

I spent the day enjoying the present and reflecting on my hike: The Pacific Crest Trail fit my personality. I loved my thru-hike of the Appalachian Trail but there were many day hikers, section hikers, and thru-hikers, and there was rarely the feeling of being alone in the woods. There were lots of shelters to stop for breaks or spend the night and there was a lot of socializing. I spent most of the day saying: "Hi. How are ya?" to hikers on the Trail.

On the Pacific Crest Trail, many times, the only people I saw during the day were thru-hikers and usually not many of them. There were times I would hike one or two days and not see one person. To be completely alone, without any human distractions, totally immersed in my surroundings – those are memories I cherish.

Often on the Appalachian Trail I was enclosed in the forest. I never used suntan lotion. On the Pacific Crest Trail I spent a lot of time hiking on the sides or on top of mountains. I could look for miles and not see signs of civilization. I loved that. I used tubes of suntan lotion on the Pacific Crest Trail and still had a dark tan. I was as dark as I have ever been by the end of the desert. Over the years I camped many nights alone. There was always a tiny tinge of anxiety as I listened for sounds in the night. For the first time, on the Pacific Crest Trail, that anxiety was gone. I felt relaxed and completely at peace with my surroundings. After a full day of hiking, I slept soundly. The Appalachian Trail turned my body into a hiking machine. On the Pacific Crest Trail my conditioning was even better. It had to be. I hiked the Appalachian Trail in 148 days. I hiked the Pacific Crest Trail in 149 days. The Pacific Crest Trail is 482 miles longer than the Appalachian Trail. From Idyllwild, California at mile 178, I had to push hard all the way to the end. I could never coast like I could at the end of my Appalachian Trail hike. To be in peak physical condition felt great. Chimney Sweep, Lorax, and I spent three hours climbing a high mountain. We were hiking fast and deeply engrossed in conversation. I'm sure our heart rates were up but we weren't even breathing hard. There were places on the Pacific Crest Trail that were spectacular: The High Sierras, Crater Lake, Knife's Edge, Tunnel Falls and surrounding area, the Glacier Peak Wilderness, the North Cascades. They left me with lifetime memories.

I had the quiet and solitude I love, but enjoyed being part of the hiking community. I couldn't have been happier with my thru-hike of the Pacific Crest Trail.

It had been a long, hard, journey. I had trudged 2,640 miles through hot, dry deserts, beautiful forests, to the top of countless mountains, deep into canyons, over streams, rivers, glaciers and lava flows, around volcanoes, next to waterfalls and glistening lakes. Now I had less than twenty miles to go. The Trail was tricky at times and I kept telling myself: "Don't pull a Gourmet!"

I had to plan much more for the Pacific Crest Trail than for the Appalachian Trail. I read Yogi's Handbooks over and over before starting my hike. She listed the towns where I would be stopping for resupply and had pictures of some of the places along the Trail. I looked at pictures of Eagle Rock, Forrester Pass, the Los Angeles Aqueduct, Crater Lake, and Stehekin.

She listed names of towns and places, like Warner Springs, Paradise View Café, Idyllwild, Cajon Pass, Mojave, Kennedy Meadows, Vermillion Valley Resort, Tuolumne Meadows, Echo Lake, Sierra City, Chester, Drakesbad Guest Ranch, Etna, Seiad Valley Café, Crater Lake, Timberline Lodge, Cascade Locks, Snoqualmie, Skykomish, Stehekin, and the monument at the border.

When I was planning my hike I would read about these towns and places and daydream: I wonder if I will see Eagle Rock? I wonder if I will make it all the way to Mojave, California? What will the desert be like? Will I see a wind farm with giant wind turbines? I wonder if I will make it to Kennedy Meadows? What will the High Sierras be like? Will there be snow at Forrester Pass? I wonder if I will get to Timberline Lodge and have the all you can eat breakfast? Will I make it to Canada?

As I hiked along on this warm, lovely day, it was fun running through my checklist:

Eagle Rock – Check

Mojave (Town and Desert) – Check

Wind Farms and Wind Turbines – UGH!

Kennedy Meadows – Check

High Sierras –Gorgeous! – Double Check

Forrester Pass (Just a tiny patch of snow) – Check

Timberline Lodge (All you can eat breakfast) – Burp! – Double Check

Now I was down to my final goal – the monument at the Canadian Border. I took out my GPS and watched it count down to six miles before the border. I was curious to see where Gourmet fell. At the six mile mark there was an uneven area with sand and loose rocks. I took my time and cautiously walked over it. With about a mile to go I was greeted by some southbound hikers. They were super enthusiastic and cheered me on. I picked up the pace. It was almost dark and I was looking for a long, narrow, clear cut that marked the border. I turned a corner and there it was! I was the only person there. I went over and touched the monument. For the last

2,482 miles there was an intense focus to reach my goal. When I touched the monument I could feel the pressure evaporate, leaving me with a feeling of happiness and pride.

The end had a gentle feel to it. I knew nothing could compete with finishing the Appalachian Trail atop Katahdin with my brother, so I didn't try. There was a camping spot on the Canadian side and I headed to it. Blackbeard and Destroyer had a campfire going. We congratulated each other. I set up my tent and headed back to the campfire. It was getting cold. The campfire felt good. We sat and happily reminisced for the next half hour. I was glad to be finished and sharing this moment with these good people.

ABOUT THE AUTHOR

Jim Hill is an avid backpacker who lives in Rio Rancho, New Mexico. He has another book on thru-hiking called: "Appalachian Adventure".